NOEL R. BAGWELL, III, ESQ.

HOW TO STRUCTURE YOUR BUSINESS FOR SUCCESS

CHOOSING THE CORRECT LEGAL STRUCTURE FOR YOUR BUSINESS

THIRD EDITION

FRONT MATTER

LEGAL NOTICE

COPYRIGHT

ISBN: 978-1-0878-7887-4 (Hardcover)
ISBN: 978-1-0878-7888-1 (EPUB)

Library of Congress Control Number: 2020907209

Front cover image by trashhand
Book design by Noel Bagwell

Printed by IngramSpark in the United States of America.

Third Edition 2020. First printing edition 2020.

Executive Legal Professionals, PLLC ("ExecutiveLP®")
3102 West End Ave, STE 400
Nashville, TN 37203-1623

https://ExecutiveLP.com/

TABLE OF CONTENTS

PREFACE

THE IMPORTANCE OF CHOOSING CAREFULLY

Making a decision to start or change the structure of an existing a business is difficult, and one of the most challenging aspects of that decision is choosing the proper business form, or legal structure, the business will take. The choice of business form has a powerful impact on what legal and tax ramifications the business will experience. However, consideration of what form one's business should take should not stop at the twin pillars of Legal Liability and Tax Liability.

Though many acknowledge the legal and tax implications of various business forms, most tend to overlook or quickly gloss over the various structural benefits and potential organizational pitfalls associated with each category of business organization. While it may seem boring or tedious, to some, nevertheless acquiring at least some understanding of the various types of business structures[1] available is important for each business owner. In the end, the better one understands these issues, the more informed his final decision will be.

The following sections of this brief Preface are aimed at providing a baseline of knowledge from which to launch your exploration of introductory-to-intermediate business organization issues. Nothing in this eBook is intended to be a substitute for the advice of a licensed attorney in your jurisdiction, and the authors strongly urge you to hire an attorney to advise you regarding any decisions that could affect your legal rights.

---

[1] The terms "business structures," or "structures," and the term "business organizations," or "organizations," are used interchangeably throughout this eBook. See also the Glossary of Terms, "Business Organizations".

BUSINESS ORGANIZATIONS IN A NUTSHELL

There are, generally speaking, six different types of businesses: sole proprietorships, cooperatives, partnerships, limited liability companies, S-Corporations, and C-Corporations. Of course, one might point out that S- and C-Corporations really are both variations on the same general form of business (a corporation), or one might argue that there are any number of variations of partnerships or LLCs not listed, here. With a deferential nod to the contrarian, the author begs your indulgence.

The first form of business, the Sole Proprietorship, is the least costly to create. One usually only needs to acquire a business license, if required by the locality in which the business will operate, and make its goods or services available to the public. Next up on the organizational complexity scale is a Partnership. Partnerships involve two or more people, each having at least a 1% ownership stake in the business. Partnerships can limit the liability of minority partners, but there must always be one General Partner who is 100% liable for all the debts and obligations of the Partnership. Both Sole Proprietorships and Partnerships are taxed as "pass through" entities, meaning each partner pays taxes as an individual, and the income of the business, itself, is not taxed at the federal level.

Finally, LLCs and S- and C-Corporations, while costly to form and operate, can provide some—and often substantial—liability protection to those who own and operate such companies. LLCs and S-Corporations can be structured as pass-through entities, but C-Corporations cannot. The greatest benefit of organized or incorporated companies, beyond their legal liability and tax liability benefits, is the strength and flexibility of their hierarchy. Such company structures are designed for growth, collaboration, and capital generation. While forming a company is not always necessary for every business, certain benefits—and costs—accrue to companies that are unavailable to other businesses, making them desirable for many businesses.

ORGANIZATIONAL COMPLEXITY VS. RISK OF PERSONAL LIABILITY

In addition to the legal and tax aspects of each type of business structure, there are also organizational issues to consider from a "corporate operations" perspective—that is, from the perspective of what it takes to create, maintain, and eventually wind up the entity that operates a business. Operating a sole proprietorship on a day-to-day basis is relatively simple and intuitive. Sole proprietorships are not required to hold corporate meetings, account to shareholders, or maintain official records for reporting purposes (except such records as are required for tax reporting). By contrast, operating a corporation is far more complex, for the law imposes very strict requirements that must be met in order to carry on daily business.

Nevertheless, while structuring a business as a sole proprietorship might seem like the best choice in terms of organizational simplicity, there are also potential disadvantages associated with this business organization, such as unlimited legal liability. An owner of a sole proprietorship enjoys no separation between their personal and business identities, for the actions of the business itself are always those of the business's owner-operator. If a sole proprietorship defaults on a business loan or causes harm to its consumers through the sale of a defective product, then the owner is personally responsible for these liabilities.

For sole proprietorships, there is simply no legal distinction between business and personal actions, and the same is true for business and personal property. While general partnerships allow this responsibility to be spread out evenly among two or more partners, at the end of the day, the similar rules apply— actions taken, debts incurred, or liabilities attributable to the partnership business are likewise imputed to its owners on a joint and several basis.[2]

By contrast, even though corporations and limited liability companies may be more complex in terms of day-to-day operations, the added benefit of these structures is the additional degree of separation that exists between the business and its owners. Instead of attributing the actions of the business to the owners themselves, the state allows the actions of those authorized to act on behalf of the business to confer liability only upon the business, and not those individual people acting on its behalf. Therefore, there is less risk of such actions being imputed to a business's owners, personally.

---

[2] See Glossary, "Joint and Several Liability".

While ease of operation is certainly a key factor to consider, it's also important to understand the close correlation between organizational simplicity and greater legal liability. Although a higher degree of organizational complexity may seem like a deterrent to starting a new business, one of the primary benefits associated with more complex business organizations, like LLCs and corporations, is reduced personal liability for the owners. Given the inverse relationship between two issues, it's important for business owners to consider each in determining the proper structure for their business.

ENTITY VS. NON-ENTITY STRUCTURES

Recall the types of business organizations mentioned in this Preface's "Business Organizations in a Nutshell" section. Each business organization occupies a separate and distinct position when viewed along a non-entity–entity spectrum.

The preceding diagram portrays each type of business organization along an entity spectrum. The term "entity," in a legal context, refers to a legal fiction—a person that legally exists, but is not a natural person, and which has certain legal rights and obligations, although it does not have all the rights a natural person has. Non-entity organizations exhibit little to no separation between the business and its owners, whereas the owners of entity structures are viewed as entirely separate and distinct from the business itself.

On the far left of the spectrum, sole proprietorships and general partnerships can easily be classified as non-entity structures. The characteristics of non-entity structures typically include unlimited personal liability for owners and limited lifespan. Owners are not required to formally register these businesses with a governmental entity, and the businesses themselves are not subject to separate taxation apart from their owners. At least for the most part, sole proprietorships and general partnerships are considered legally inseparable from their owners.

Positioned near the center of the entity spectrum, limited partnerships, limited liability partnerships, and limited liability companies each possess both entity and non-entity characteristics, and in varying degrees. Though not always the case, these businesses are typically required to meet at least some type of formal registration requirements prior to conducting business. For purposes of taxation, limited partnerships and limited liability partnerships are best characterized as non-entities, given that partnership businesses are not taxed separately from their owners or partners. While owners or members of LLCs can elect to have their businesses taxed at the entity level, this is a fairly uncommon practice. As such, LLCs are most commonly taxed as non-entities and are not required to file separate tax returns from their owners.

When it comes to liability, members in an LLC typically enjoy a greater degree of protection from personal liability than partners in limited and limited liability partnerships. This, of course, may change depending on how each partner is classified in relation to the partnership, as well as the specific type of liability at issue. Aside from certain exceptions, personal liability for the owners of these types of businesses is more characteristic of a non-entity structure, and actions undertaken in the ordinary course business are generally not attributable to the owners on a personalized basis.

Located on the far right of the spectrum, corporations enjoy near complete separation from their owners. These businesses are viewed as entirely distinct from their owners in nearly every way. To that end, corporations can sue and be sued by others, they can hold property, exercise separate constitutional rights to free speech, own and hold stock or equity in other business, as well as a variety of other things that other non-entity structures simply cannot. Unlike other types of business structures, corporations also have the ability to exist forever, as their continued existence is not dependent on the lives of their individual owners to remain intact.

Economics, the science of human decision-making, gives us a fundamental rule one should keep in mind, when making any decision—especially one as crucial as which business organization to choose for your business. The rule is simple, but its implications are vast. The rule is this: "All decisions are made at the margins."

One should ask himself: do I need *marginally more* or *marginally less* liability limitation; do I need *marginally more* simplicity (or complexity), or *marginally less* simplicity (or complexity); do I need *marginally more* or *marginally less* of this, that, or the other thing. Do not fall into the trap of all-or-nothing thinking.

Additionally, be careful not to over-value (or under-value) any single aspect of a business organization. For example, some people are attracted to corporations, because they feel like a big shot when they put "Business Name, **Inc.**" on a business card. This sort of hollow puffery is as transparent as it is pathetic, and could easily make one the butt of a joke among seasoned executives, investors, and entrepreneurs. The mantra, "Fake it 'till you make it," is bullshit, especially when it comes to wholly substantive matters, such as what business organization you choose. This is not a decision you should make based on appearances or other ways of superficially posturing.

Similarly, avoid making your decision solely on the basis of the perceived tax implications of your decision. While taxes are one important issue to consider, they're far from the *only* issue. Don't be like the single-issue voter who casts his ballot for whichever candidate with whom he agrees on his pet issue, while disregarding the rest of the candidate's platform. Being focused on what is important is admirable, but having tunnel vision is not. Perspicacity requires a degree of peripheral vision in one's business affairs.

Focus on the essential. If you need help doing this, or don't feel extremely confident in your ability to sort, and keep your efforts focused on, only the most essential things, before reading the rest of this book, you should read *Essentialism*, by Greg McKeown.

Whatever you do, don't rush into this decision, and don't make it alone. Talk to a lawyer and an accountant, at least, before you make a decision. And for the love of all that is good and holy, don't <u>try to DIY your legal work</u>. Good luck!

DISCLAIMER REGARDING TAX INFORMATION

The author of this book is not a tax attorney. The tax-related information provided herein is not in any way comprehensive, and is probably incomplete. This is not a book about taxation of business organizations. Briefly, taxation issues may be mentioned during discussions of each type of business organization, but the author has no intent to attempt to treat such issues with the degree of attention or thoroughness they deserve. Rather, he leaves that to other professionals whose practices focus on those issues, and encourages you, in the strongest possible terms, to seek out such individuals, and consult with them before making decisions that could impact your tax-related legal rights!

While every attempt to ensure the scant tax-related information provided herein is accurate, the author makes no guarantee that it is accurate or up-to-date. So, please be extremely cautious and skeptical, and do not make decisions based on the tax-related information included in this book. Such information is provided here, for your convenience, because the author wants to help you gain, at least, *his level of understanding* of these issues, while simultaneously acknowledging that a deeper level of understanding may be required in order to make the best decision in your unique circumstances.

Do not rely exclusively on the tax-related information in this book!

CHAPTER ONE

SOLE PROPRIETORSHIPS

As stated in the Preface, the Sole Proprietorship, is the least costly to create (one's parents already did the hard work for him). There is no difference between a sole proprietorship and the business's owner (the "sole proprietor" or, simply, "proprietor").

Proprietors are not required to formally register their business with any governmental entity in order to bring the sole proprietorship into existence. One usually only needs to acquire a business license, if required by the state, county, or city in which the business will operate and make its goods or services available to the public.

There are a few things you can do to add the more formal trappings of a business to your sole proprietorship. Registering a trade name and getting an Employer Identification Number (EIN) from the Internal Revenue Service (I.R.S.) are good ways to increase your business's "footprint" on paper. Of course, like any business, a sole proprietorship should maintain separate business accounts for operations, payroll, etc.

Having both an accountant and a business lawyer as part of your team are essential, even if you cannot afford to put either on your payroll. An attorney who serves as "general counsel" is the chief lawyer for a business; if that lawyer is independently contracted, and not on the business's payroll, he is said to be "outside general counsel" for the business. Outside general counsel services are crucial to a business's success, because legal services are necessary for every business, and are one area where cutting corners will usually result in expensive problems later. Taking a proactive, preventive approach to your legal issues may, at first, seem costly, but the preventive approach is often far less expensive than the alternative—litigation. Your business will also need an accountant for similar reasons. It's better to pay a little for bookkeeping services in advance than pay a lot when you get audited, later.

Often, an important aspect of operating a sole proprietorship is establishing a strong trade name that will be the most visible part of the business's brand. A sole proprietor can use a trade name, for example, "Nashville Guitar and Penguin Emporium." Legally, the business is just the person—the sole proprietor—who operates it. So, all legal documents, contracts, etc. would provide the businesses name as something like: "Johnny Derp d/b/a Nashville Guitar and Penguin Emporium." The "d/b/a" means "doing business as," and is used whenever a person or business is doing business under a trade name. Both sole proprietors and organized businesses can use trade names.

There really isn't much more to creating a sole proprietorship than that. One thing that should be mentioned, in addition to reiterating the need for having both outside general counsel and a CPA on your team, is the necessity of a written business plan. A business without a written business plan is like an ancient sailing ship on the high seas without a map. It might be a sunny day with wind in your sails when you start out, but a storm is coming, and you're going to get tossed around a bit. You better have a way to figure out where you are when that happens. A well-written, thorough business plan will keep you oriented on your priorities and help you stay on track, come what may.

FEDERAL INCOME TAX ISSUES FOR SOLE PROPRIETORSHIPS

"Because you and your business are one and the same, the business itself is not taxed separately—the sole proprietorship income is your income. You report income and/or losses and expenses with a Schedule C and the standard Form 1040. The 'bottom-line amount' from Schedule C transfers to your personal tax return. It's your responsibility to withhold and pay all income taxes, including self-employment and estimated taxes. You can find more information about sole proprietorship taxes and other forms at IRS.gov."[3]

---

[3] U.S. Small Business Administration (2020). Sole Proprietorship. Retrieved January 3, 2020, from https://www.sba.gov/content/sole-proprietorship.

STATE-LEVEL TAX ON PASS-THROUGH BUSINESSES (TENNESSEE)

Tennessee imposes a 6.5% income tax and a 0.25% net worth tax on limited liability companies, limited partnerships, and limited liability partnerships.[4] The franchise tax is imposed at a rate of .25% of the greater of net worth or real and tangible property in Tennessee or the $100 minimum tax.[5]

Tennessee does not impose these taxes on sole proprietorships, however, because franchise and excise taxes are imposed upon the privilege of doing business in the state and are not laid upon corporate earnings, in the sense that an income tax is so laid, but are measured entirely by the net income of the business entity.[6] Moreover, to be clear, franchise and excise taxes were laid upon the privilege of engaging in business in corporate form in Tennessee and not merely upon the doing of business.[7]

California, Illinois, Kentucky, Michigan, New Hampshire, New Jersey, New York, Ohio, Texas, and Washington, as well as the District of Columbia, all impose an entity-level taxes, of one kind or another, on pass-through businesses. If your business is conducted in one of the above-listed states, please consult with a local tax attorney or CPA to determine the applicability and compliance requirements of any such tax. At the time of this writing, no other states presently impose an entity-level tax on pass-throughs.

---

[4] Tenn. Code Ann. §§ 67-4-201, 67-4-2007, 67-4-2105.

[5] Tenn. Code Ann. §§ 67-4-2007, 67-4-2106.

[6] *Roane Hosiery, Inc. v. King*, 214 Tenn. 441, 381 S.W.2d 265, 1964 Tenn. LEXIS 492 (Tenn. July 15, 1964). Cf.

[7] *Mid-Valley Pipeline Co. v. King*, 221 Tenn. 724, 431 S.W.2d 277, 1968 Tenn. LEXIS 532 (1968), appeal dismissed, 393 U.S. 321, 89 S. Ct. 556, 21 L. Ed. 2d 517, 1969 U.S. LEXIS 2869 (1969), appealed dismissed, *Mid-Valley Pipeline Co. v. King*, 393 U.S. 321, 89 S. Ct. 556, 21 L. Ed. 2d 517, 1969 U.S. LEXIS 2869 (1969).

FINAL THOUGHTS: SOLE PROPRIETORSHIPS

Tennessee imposes a 6.5% income tax and a 0.25% net worth tax on limited liability companies, limited partnerships, and limited liability partnerships.[8] The franchise tax is imposed at a rate of .25% of the greater of net worth or real and tangible property in Tennessee or the $100 minimum tax. These taxes do not apply to sole proprietorships. Additionally, property of a sole proprietorship that becomes property of a corporation (or LLC) as a result of incorporation (or organization) of the sole proprietorship is not subject to tax. Tenn. Code Ann. § 67-6-223.

Sole proprietorships are the least expensive types of business organizations to begin operating, because all that is required to start a sole proprietorship is for an individual to start conducting business. In order to operate a business in most local jurisdictions (cities, counties, etc.), the business will need to obtain a business license. This applies equally to sole proprietorships and other kinds of entities. So, sole proprietorships are not without some start-up costs—even regulatory compliance costs. Other rules, such as worker's compensation regulations, wage & hour laws, and the like also apply to sole proprietorships, though, in some circumstances, to a lesser degree than to larger businesses.

Most people focus too much on the fact that sole proprietors have unlimited personal liability for the debts and legal liabilities of the business, and ignore the benefits that arise from this light, versatile structure. Don't dismiss it out of hand.

---

[8] Tenn. Code Ann. §§ 67-4-201, 67-4-2007, 67-4-2105.

CHAPTER TWO

PARTNERSHIPS, GENERALLY

A partnership, in many ways, is like a marriage. In each case, the two parties are treated as one. This is the best way to understand the concept of joint and several liability. In a partnership, the partners, like spouses, are considered one, for legal purposes. If one gets sued, the other has liability, and vice versa.

If a claimant (or "plaintiff") cannot serve all the partners of a partnership, they may or may not be able to recover the full amount owed to them, depending on whether or not the partners are entitled to liability limitation, under state law. In a General Partnership, the partners' joint and several liability is unlimited. So, if a plaintiff sues the General Partnership, they can collect up to 100% from *any one partner*; the plaintiff only has to be able to reach one partner, and their assets, in order to recover.

In a limited partnership, there is at least one general partner (with unlimited joint and several liability) and a number of limited partners, each of which enjoy limited (proportional) liability, according to the amount of Partnership Interest in the partnership that each partner holds. In a limited liability partnership, each partner enjoys limited (proportional) liability, according to the amount of Partnership Interest in the partnership that each partner holds.

Additionally, if one or more partners are held liable for the debts, or legal liabilities, of the partnership, but others are not, a claim may arise between partners for contribution. Below is a discussion of example scenarios involving various partnership liabilities. Contribution will be described more fully, and the incidence of a claim for contribution is illustrated, in one of the following examples.

The important thing to remember is that liability for limited partners is proportional, and exists in proportion to the total percentage of Partnership Interests they hold. General partners, however, have joint and several liability, and each general partner can be held liable for up to 100% of the debts or obligations of the partnership.

Example 1: General Partnership

Two partners, Jim Hanson and Kermit Defraug d/b/a Acme Widget Supply (a general partnership), have a dispute with their supplier, Miss P. Iggy, over an invoice. Miss P. Iggy sues Acme Widget Supply, and the two partners thereof, for breach of contract, and wins a judgment for $10,000.00.

The Partnership Interest Mr. Hanson holds is 80% of the total Partnership Interests in Acme Widget Supply; so, he is responsible to pay $8,000.00 **or** up to $10,000.00 if the entire $2,000.00 balance cannot be collected from Mr. Defraug, who holds 20% of the Partnership Interests in the business. If Mr. Defraug pays less than $2,000.00 to Miss P. Iggy, then Mr. Hanson must pay Miss P. Iggy and collect from Mr. Defraug's contribution—the portion he paid Miss P. Iggy on Mr. Defraug's behalf—in a separate legal action. Likewise, if Miss P. Iggy can collect 100% from Mr. Defraug, but not Mr. Hanson, then Mr. Defraug can collect the balance of up to $8,000 in contribution from Mr. Hanson.

Example 2: Limited Partnership

Jim Hanson and Kermit Defraug d/b/a Acme Widget Supply (a limited partnership), have a dispute with their supplier, Miss P. Iggy, over an invoice. Miss P. Iggy sues Acme Widget Supply, and the two partners thereof, for breach of contract, and wins a judgment for $10,000.00.

The Partnership Interest Mr. Hanson holds is 80% of the total Partnership Interests in Acme Widget Supply, and he is a General Partner; so, he is responsible to pay $8,000.00 **or** up to $10,000.00 if the entire $2,000.00 balance cannot be collected from Mr. Defraug, who, as a limited partner, holds 20% of the Partnership Interests in the business. If Mr. Defraug pays less than $2,000.00 to Miss P. Iggy, then Mr. Hanson must pay Miss P. Iggy and collect from Mr. Defraug's contribution—the portion he paid Miss P. Iggy on Mr. Defraug's behalf—in a separate legal action. However, if Miss P. Iggy can collect only from Mr. Defraug, but not Mr. Hanson, then Mr. Defraug can only be held liable for up to $2,000.00 (20% of $10,000, a proportionate share of liability, which matches his proportion of Partnership Interest holdings).

Example 3: Limited Liability Partnership

Jim Hanson and Kermit Defraug d/b/a Acme Widget Supply (a limited liability partnership), have a dispute with their supplier, Miss P. Iggy, over an invoice. Miss P. Iggy sues Acme Widget Supply, and the two partners thereof, for breach of contract, and wins a judgment for $10,000.00.

The Partnership Interest Mr. Hanson holds is 80% of the total Partnership Interests in Acme Widget Supply, and he is a limited partner; so, he is responsible to pay $8,000.00, regardless of whether or not the $2,000.00 balance can be collected from Mr. Defraug, who, as a limited partner, holds 20% of the Partnership Interests in the business. Likewise, if Miss P. Iggy can collect only from Mr. Defraug, but not Mr. Hanson, then Mr. Defraug can only be held liable for up to $2,000.00.

TYPES OF PARTNERSHIPS

In most jurisdictions, there are generally three major kinds of partnerships: General Partnerships (GPs), Limited Partnerships (LPs), and Limited-Liability Partnerships (LLPs). In a GP, each partner usually participates in the management of the business and has unlimited liability for the debts and obligations of the business. If one partner is sued, all partners are held jointly and severally liable. Unlike a GP, an LP limits the liability of holders of minority interests in the partnership–often referred to as "limited partners" or "limited liability partners"– but there still must always be at least one general partner who has unlimited liability for the debts and obligations of the business. In an LLP, the liability of all partners is limited to some extent. LLPs operate similar to limited-liability companies (LLCs), which will be discussed in a subsequent section of this paper.

When forming a partnership, one should have a clear reason for structuring it one way as opposed to another. For example, if three potential partners come together to form a partnership, and two are not going to participate in the management of the business, but are going to provide start-up capital and ongoing credit to the business while the other manages the day-to-day operations of the business, a limited partnership is likely to be the best structure for that partnership. If two or more partners are all going to be involved in the management of the business, a general partnership or LLP may be preferable, depending on the nature of the business. The choice of the kind of partnership you form should be based on the incentives and concerns of the various partners. If you are uncertain about which form of partnership would be best for your venture, you should consult a business attorney.

FORMING A PARTNERSHIP: WHAT NOT TO DO

In the case of *Summers v. Dooley*, 481 P.2d 318 (Idaho 1971), a man named Summers entered into a partnership agreement with another named Dooley to operate a trash collection business. The two men operated the business together, and each supplied a temporary replacement if the other was unable to work. About eight years into the partnership, Summers approached his partner, Dooley, about hiring an additional employee, but Dooley refused. Nevertheless, on his own initiative, Summers hired the man and paid him out of his own pocket. Dooley, upon discovering Summers had hired an additional man, objected, stating he did not feel additional labor was necessary.

Dooley refused to pay for the new employee out of the partnership's funds. Summers continued to operate the business using the third man, and, the next year, filed a lawsuit against his partner for $6,000.00.

The issue in *Summers v. Dooley* was whether an equal partner in a two-man partnership has the authority to hire a new employee in disregard of the objection of the other partner and then attempt to charge the dissenting partner with the costs incurred as a result of his unilateral decision. The court held that, if partners are equally divided, those who forbid a change must have their way, citing Walter B. Lindley's *A Treatise on the Law of Partnership*, Ch. II, § III, ¶ 24-8, p. 403 (1924).

The court noted that Dooley continually voiced objection to the hiring of the third man. He did not sit idly by and acquiesce in the actions of his partner. Under such circumstances, the court found, it would have been manifestly unjust to permit Summers to recover an expense which was incurred individually and not for the benefit of the partnership, per se, but rather for the benefit of one partner.

Summers v. Dooley is a classic partnership law case, because it illustrates not just the principle for which it is generally cited–that if partners are equally divided, those who forbid a change must have their way–but, more broadly, the potentially complex dynamics of even a two-man "50/50" partnership. A well-drafted Partnership Agreement is essential to a smoothly-run partnership, because it will specify under what circumstances each partner has authority to act on behalf of the partnership. Partnerships can exist without a Partnership Agreement, but operating a partnership without a written Partnership is foolish.

WHAT A PARTNERSHIP AGREEMENT ACTUALLY DOES

A partner relationship is generally the result of a contract either express or implied with no formal requirements (such as a signed document). To determine whether a partnership exists courts look at: (1) intention of the parties, (2) sharing of profits and losses (3) joint administration and control of business operation, (4) capital investment by each partner, and (5) common ownership of property. Ask yourself whether you trust a court to accurately interpret the intentions potential partners and to correctly determine each and every one of those 5 elements.

Now, ask yourself whether you would prefer to have a contract that clearly and comprehensively discusses each of those elements with respect to a potential partnership. That is what a partnership agreement does. The benefits are obvious, and practically universally outweigh the costs of having a Partnership Agreement drafted by a business attorney.

OTHER CONSIDERATIONS WHEN FORMING A PARTNERSHIP

Every partnership will have an interest in establishing a strong trade name, often the most visible part of a business's brand aside from its logo. For some partnerships, the name is just the names of the senior partners all together. Partnerships, however, like other organized businesses, can use trade names that do not include the names of the partners. Registering your partnership's trade name with the Secretary of State in the state in which you do business may be necessary. In some states, like Tennessee, it is not necessary to register your partnership's trade name with the Secretary of State, but it may still be desirable to do so. You should consult a business attorney to help you make this decision.

There are a few things you can do to add the more formal trappings to a business when forming a partnership. Getting an Employer Identification Number (EIN) from the Internal Revenue Service (I.R.S.) is a good way to increase your business's "footprint" on paper. A partnership will want to use the EIN to open bank accounts and other accounts in the name of the business. Of course, like any business, a partnership should maintain separate business accounts for operations, payroll, etc.

Having both an accountant and a business lawyer as part of your team are essential, even if you cannot afford to put either on your payroll. An attorney who serves as "general counsel" is the chief lawyer for a business; if that lawyer is independently contracted, and not on the business's payroll, he is said to be "outside general counsel" for the business. Outside general counsel services are crucial to a business's success, because legal services are necessary for every business, and are one area where cutting corners will usually result in expensive problems later. Taking a proactive, preventive approach to your legal issues can seem costly, but the preventive approach is often far less expensive than the alternative—litigation. Obviously, unless you're a CPA, you also need an accountant for similar reasons. It's better to pay a little for bookkeeping services in advance than pay a lot when you get audited, later.

In addition to reiterating the need for having both outside general counsel and a CPA on your team, is the necessity of a written business plan. A business without a written business plan is like an ancient sailing ship on the high seas without a map. It might be a sunny day with wind in your sails when you start out, but a storm is coming, and you're going to get tossed around a bit. You better have a way to figure out where you are when that happens. A well-written, thorough business plan will keep you oriented on your priorities and help you stay on track, come what may.

GENERAL PARTNERSHIPS

General partnerships, like sole proprietorships, are pass-through or "disregarded" entities. The primary difference between partnerships and sole proprietorships is that, obviously, there is always more than one business owner. A general partnership is simply a voluntary association of two or more persons for carrying on a business as co-owners for profit.

General partnerships have a few less obvious characteristics that sole proprietorships do not, as well, such as the ability to hold property and maintain lawsuits in the name of the partnership. Just like an owner of a sole proprietorship, however, partners in a general partnership remain personally responsible for all debts and liabilities of the partnership business.

Consider a boy who decides to form a partnership with his sister to operate their lemonade stand. The siblings agree to carry on the business as co-owners for a profit. By pooling their collective allowances, to use as start-up capital, they are able to buy more supplies for the business. Brother and sister agree that profits will be split fifty-fifty, as will any debts and liabilities arising in connection with the business.

General partnerships do not enjoy separate legal existence from their owners. There are no requirements to formally register the partnership prior to engaging in business operations. Consequently, all profits and losses of the business, as well as debts and liabilities incurred by the business, are subject, by default, to a *pro rata* split amongst the separate partners. A written Partnership Agreement, however, may establish a different split of both profits and liabilities.

Likewise, each partner possesses decision-making and management authority over the business in proportion to their share of ownership, unless otherwise provided by the Partnership Agreement. Returning to our lemonade stand example, in the absence of a Partnership Agreement, brother and sister would each have an equal say in how their business should operate. All decisions affecting the partnership must be decided upon collectively, though day-to-day operational decisions affecting the lemonade stand may be delegated to either partner, or even an employee or independent contractor. If disagreements arise between the two partners, the dissenting partner–the one wanting to maintain the *status quo*–will always get their way. Therefore, using the Partnership Agreement to establish a determinative dispute resolution process, *before a dispute arises*, is of paramount importance.

An interesting dilemma for general partnership structures arises when one partner enters into a contract with a third party without the other's knowledge or consent. If a partner creates such a liability in the ordinary course of business, and obtains and uses the benefits pertaining thereto in furtherance of the same, then joint and several liability arises for all partners. Of course, if a partner creates a liability outside the scope of the partnership, such as a loan to cover personal expenses, then he alone would be responsible for the liability or obligation.

One would do well to notice that the general partnership structure provides no protection for any partner's personal assets. If the assets of the business prove insufficient to cover any debts, obligations, or liabilities arising in connection with the partnership, the personal assets of any partner may be seized and sold to cover the debts, obligations, or liabilities of the business. Each partner shares unlimited liability for actions of the partnership as a whole if a number of partners less than the total number of partners can be held to account for the partnership's debts, obligations, or liabilities. As such, if a general partnership structure is something you're considering, pay close attention to how you will be impacted by joint and several liability.

LIMITED PARTNERSHIPS

A limited partnership is a partnership that consists of at least one general partner and one or more limited partners. The general partner manages the partnership's business, and they have unlimited personal liability for all the debts and obligations of the partnership. Limited partners, on the other hand, have limited liability, but they cannot control the management of the business.

Most states have adopted some version of the Uniform Limited Partnership Act (ULPA), but, perhaps ironically, there is quite a bit of variety in the ULPA, as enacted in various jurisdictions. Most of the ULPA's provisions are meant to serve as "default rules," so to speak, and can be modified by partners through the use of a written Partnership Agreement. Just as in a general partnership, in a limited partnership, a written Partnership Agreement is highly desirable, if not strictly necessary, for customizing the structure to fit the needs of the business.

Unlike the partners in a general partnership (or limited liability partnership), limited partners usually do not participate in the control of the limited partnership. They don't usually have actual authority, and almost never have apparent authority, to act alone on the partnership's behalf. Such activities, in a limited partnership, are almost exclusively reserved for general partners. Moreover, unlike the officers and directors of a corporation, or the general partners of a general partnership, limited partners have no fiduciary duties to the partnership.

The foregoing general statements are, however, not universally applicable, for, under at least one form of the ULPA, as enacted, several safe harbors apply under which limited partners can participate in the limited partnership's business and affairs—usually by voting—without being deemed to have control of the limited partnership. In such circumstances, limited partners may only act as permitted by ULPA or the partnership agreement.

For the limited partners, the advantages of the limited partnership structure pertain to the liability shield they enjoy, provided they're complying with the ULPA and the partnership agreement.

LIMITED LIABILITY PARTNERSHIPS

Limited Liability Partnerships ("LLPs") are entities that provide for limited personal liability for all of the partners, while conducting business subject to a partnership agreement.

An LLP starts its existence as a general partnership. Then, upon compliance with statutory requirements, it obtains from the state limited liability protection for its partners. Most LLPs are operated by those providing professional services, such as legal and accounting services. While the partners all have the same legal status, in an LLP, some partners may take on distinct roles, just as they might do in a general partnership.

Partners' limited liability for tort, contract, and other acts arising out of business activities of the partnership, so long as the partnership maintains its limited liability partnership status, is the main reason why partners choose the LLP structure.

Compared to other entities, many consider the LLP to offer greater flexibility, in structure and in day-to-day operation, than corporations or limited liability companies ("LLCs"). LLPs, for example, can allocate items of income, gain, loss, deduction, and distributions pursuant to the partnership agreement (subject to the limitations of I.R.C. § 704(b).) As suggested, above, corporations don't enjoy such flexibility. Plus, like all partnerships, LLPs are disregarded entities (a.k.a. "pass-through" entities) for federal tax purposes; so, LLPs don't get hit with the double taxation imposed on C-corporations (and S-corporations and LLCs that elect to be taxed in the same way as C-corporations).

It's not all wine and roses, though. Partnerships, including LLPs, may not have the flexibility corporations enjoy, when adding equity-holders or transferring equity (partnership interest in a partnership or stock in a corporation). LLPs also tend to have fewer structural elements that stabilize more complex entities (e.g. corporations and limited liability companies). Disagreements among the partners can easily cause the dissolution of the partnership, especially in the absence of a carefully drafted Partnership Agreement. Additionally, if one or more partners commit the partnership to business agreements without the consent of the other partners, the partnership may, nevertheless, be obligated by those commitments.

Partners in an LLP are not each jointly and severally liable for all of the partnership's obligations, they remain personally liable for their own acts of malpractice or professional negligence, as well as those of any professionals under their direct supervision or control. Furthermore, they are proportionally liable for their share of the partnership's obligations, including taxes on net profits.

For assistance with registering a general partnership as an LLP, withdrawing or revoking such a registration, designating a registered agent or changing such a designation, establishing or changing the name of the LLP, or dissolving an LLP, the partners should hire an attorney to represent the partnership as its general counsel. The general counsel attorney should be tasked with handling such business-legal matters on the partnership's behalf.

FEDERAL INCOME TAX ISSUES FOR PARTNERSHIPS

I am reluctant to engage in a discussion of taxation, which is extremely complex, even for partnerships and other disregarded entities (such as LLCs and S-Corporations that elect to be taxed in the same way as partnerships). For information regarding the tax implications of using a partnership structure in your unique circumstances, please contact ExecutiveLP® through our website[9] to schedule a consultation or obtain a referral to a tax lawyer.

---

[9] Attorney advertisement.

CHAPTER THREE

LIMITED LIABILITY COMPANIES

Contrary to popular opinion—even among lawyers—limited liability companies ("LLCs") are not the most popular form of legal entity or business structure in the United States. Sole proprietorships (nonfarm) and S-corporations both significantly outnumber LLCs. There were 24,074,684 nonfarm sole proprietorships in 2013, the last year statistics were reported by the IRS.[10] That year, there were also 4,257,909 S-corporations, while LLCs numbered only 2,285,420. *Id*. In fact, there were more partnerships—general, limited, and limited liability partnerships—than LLCs. The number of partnerships was 3,460,699 in 2013. *Id*.

So, why do so many lawyers (inaccurately) say that LLCs are the most popular form of business entity?

Cynically, one might suppose that lawyers have a perverse incentive to promote the LLC structure because it's the least expensive business entity that *must* be registered with a state in order to even *exist*. Limited partnerships and limited liability partners come into existence as general partnerships, and only obtain limited liability protection by registering. Corporations of all kinds are more expensive to create and maintain than LLCs.

One might also suppose laziness would prompt lawyers, and others, to recommend LLCs over other business structures, because LLCs have features of both partnerships and corporations. Many people refer to LLCs as "hybrid entities," and push them as a "best of both worlds" kind-of solution. This is not entirely inaccurate, but it's far from the whole picture.

In short, LLCs are popular—but far from the most popular type of business entity—because they're not only extremely flexible, but member-managed LLCs offer outstanding capital-raising potential while allowing savvy business planners to avoid securities regulation. There are no solutions, however; there are only trade-

---

[10] IRS. SOI Tax Stats - Integrated Business Data, SOI Tax Stats - Integrated Business Data (n.d.). Retrieved from https://www.irs.gov/statistics/soi-tax-stats-integrated-business-data

offs.[11] LLCs just tend to have a lot of the kinds of trade-offs modern small-to-medium businesses favor, though they're far from being the one-size-fits-all or magic bullet solution that some make them out to be.

WHAT IS AN LLC?

The cut-and-dried definition of an LLC is:

"AN UNINCORPORATED FORM OF BUSINESS ORGANIZATION, SIMILAR TO A GENERAL OR LIMITED PARTNERSHIP BUT POSSESSING A LIMITED LIABILITY SHIELD THAT PROTECTS ITS OWNERS FROM LIABILITY TO THE SAME EXTENT THAT STOCKHOLDERS OF A CORPORATION ARE INSULATED FROM ITS DEBTS AND OBLIGATIONS."[12]

LLCs have certain characteristics of both corporations and partnerships or sole proprietorships, depending on the number of members in the LLC. LLCs are not corporations, though they do limit the liability of the members in a way similar to that in which corporations limit the liability of their shareholders. Unlike corporations, but like partnerships, however, LLCs can be structured to allow the pass-through of income taxation. Such legal entities are often called "flow-through entities," "pass-through entities," or "fiscally-transparent entities." "Depending on the local tax regulations, this structure can avoid dividend tax and double taxation because only owners or investors are taxed on the revenue. Technically, for tax purposes, flow-through entities are considered "non-entities" because they are not taxed; rather, taxation "flows-through" to another tax return."

One of the most important things members of an LLC should be careful not to do is to commingle their funds with those of the LLC, because doing so weakens the veil between the LLC and its members that shields the LLC's members from personal liability for the debts and obligations of the LLC. For additional information about the circumstances under which an LLC may be disregarded or liability might otherwise accrue to the members of an LLC for an LLC's debts and obligations, interested parties should consult a business attorney.

----

[11] Sowell, T. (2007). *A Conflict of Visions: Ideological Origins of Political Struggles*. New York, NY: Basic Books.

[12] See Glossary of Terms, "Limited Liability Company".

An LLC is formed when its Articles of Organization are drafted and filed with the Secretary of State in any given state or commonwealth. Sometimes, Articles of Organization are also referred to as an "LLC Certificate" or some other similar term. In any event, the Articles of Organization are not the same as the Operating Agreement, though many people tend to be confused on this point.

An LLC is governed by its Operating Agreement and, especially in the absence of a written Operating Agreement, the LLC statute in the jurisdiction in which it was formed. The Operating Agreement is the:

> "GOVERNING CONTRACT ADOPTED BY MEMBERS OF A LIMITED LIABILITY COMPANY (LLC). IT MAY BE USED TO REGULATE NEARLY ALL ASPECTS OF THE LLC'S AFFAIRS, INCLUDING HOW THE BUSINESS IS MANAGED, HOW ASSETS ARE USED AND HOW REVENUES ARE SHARED. AN OPERATING AGREEMENT WILL OVERRIDE ANY DEFAULT RULES PRESENTED BY A STATE LLC STATUTE, WHICH CONTROLS IN THE ABSENCE OF AN OPERATING AGREEMENT."[13]

It is critical that your Operating Agreement reflect the unique organizational, financial, legal, and structural aspects of your business. Using a "one-size-fits-all" or template Operating Agreement is a bad idea, because usually one size does not fit all. When deciding how you are going to spend money to start a your company, investing in a custom-drafted, carefully written Operating Agreement created by competent business attorney for your unique business is one of the best choices you can make.

In most jurisdictions within the United States, there are generally three major kinds of LLCs: LLC, PLLC, and Series LLC. In eleven states, and two autonomous regions in the U.S., the low-profit limited liability company ("L3C") is an option for social entrepreneurship businesses.[14] These states are: Illinois, Kansas, Louisiana, Maine, Michigan, Missouri, North Dakota, Rhode Island, Utah, Vermont, Wyoming and the federal jurisdictions of the Crow Indian Nation of Montana and the Oglala Sioux Tribe.

An LLC's Articles of Organization are somewhat analogous to our Declaration of Independence or a corporation's charter, whereas the Operating Agreement is

---

[13] Legal Information Institute. (2014). Operating Agreement. Retrieved January 2, 2020, from https://www.law.cornell.edu/wex/operating_agreement.

[14] See Chapter 5 for more information about Benefit Corporations and L3Cs.

analogous to the Constitution or a corporation's bylaws. The Articles of Organization are short, and spell out the basic identifying details of the LLC, whereas the Operating Agreement is a contract between the members of the company and the company, *per se*, as well as among the members, themselves.

In Tennessee (as in most other jurisdictions), the Articles of Organization are required to be filed with the state, but the Operating Agreement is not. In fact, in Tennessee, and many other states, an Operating Agreement is not strictly required, although, for a variety of reasons, it's foolish not to have one.

LLC TAXONOMY

The standard LLC is the one described above in the "What is an LLC" section of this article.

In short, PLLCs are LLCs operated by licensed professionals in states where such operations are permitted. More specifically stated:

> "A PROFESSIONAL LIMITED LIABILITY COMPANY (PLLC, P.L.L.C., OR P.L.) IS A LIMITED LIABILITY COMPANY ORGANIZED FOR THE PURPOSE OF PROVIDING PROFESSIONAL SERVICES. EXACT REQUIREMENTS OF PLLCS VARY FROM STATE TO STATE. TYPICALLY, A PLLC'S MEMBERS MUST ALL BE PROFESSIONALS PRACTICING THE SAME PROFESSION. IN ADDITION, THE LIMITATION OF PERSONAL LIABILITY OF MEMBERS DOES NOT EXTEND TO PROFESSIONAL MALPRACTICE CLAIMS."[15]

Unless you have a professional license-such as a license to practice medicine, a license to practice law, a CPA license, etc., etc.-you should not consider forming a PLLC. Some jurisdictions, like California, do not permit LLCs to practice a licensed profession. For additional information about whether a PLLC is right for your business please consult a business attorney.

A Series LLC is sometimes chosen by asset investors, like real estate investors, because the unique Series LLC structure "allows a single LLC to segregate its assets into separate series. For example, a series LLC that purchases separate pieces of real estate may put each in a separate series so if the lender forecloses

---

[15] Americans for Community Development. "L3C Concept." Concept. Americans for Community Development, n.d. Web. 05 Aug. 2014.

on one piece of property, the others are not affected."4 Typically, a Series LLC is not going to be ideal for the average business owner and is selected only by investors in large, individually expensive-and sometimes volatile-assets.

The low-profit limited liability company ("L3C") form was designed for "use as a potential vehicle for any definable revenue stream generated for a socially beneficial purpose." Social entrepreneurship firms are what many first think of when they think of L3Cs. There are relatively few L3Cs in operation in the U.S., and it is a comparatively "young" form of LLC, the first one having been formed in Vermont in 2008. According to the Americans for Community Development:

> "THE L3C EMBODIES THE OPERATING EFFICIENCIES OF A FOR-PROFIT COMPANY ALONG WITH A REDUCED REGULATORY STRUCTURE. AS AN LLC, IT CAN BRING TOGETHER FOUNDATIONS, TRUSTS, ENDOWMENT FUNDS, PENSION FUNDS, INDIVIDUALS, CORPORATIONS, OTHER FOR-PROFITS AND GOVERNMENT ENTITIES INTO AN ORGANIZATION DESIGNED TO ACHIEVE SOCIAL OBJECTIVES WHILE ALSO OPERATING ACCORDING TO FOR-PROFIT METRICS."16

The L3C is not going to be a great fit for many companies, but for those who focus on doing well by doing good-and for those who make program-related investments ("PRIs") in such companies-the L3C can be an exceptionally beneficial business structure. The question you should ask yourself is: which is your focus-making a profit or accomplishing some socially beneficial purpose while, at least, breaking even from your enterprise's primary revenue stream?

WHY AND HOW TO FORM AN LLC

The best reason to consider forming an LLC vs. forming a corporation, partnership, or some other form of business, is because of the flexible, yet resilient, structure of the LLC form. An LLC's Articles of Organization, and to a greater extent its Operating Agreement, can clearly define many different roles and positions within your business. If you simply need to maximize the limitation of your liability, you may prefer a corporation. If you simply want an extremely

---

16 Americans for Community Development. "L3C Concept." Concept. Americans for Community Development, n.d. Web. 05 Aug. 2014.

nimble pass-through taxation entity, a partnership or an LLP might be a better choice for you. If, however, you need to

balance your competing interests in remaining nimble while achieving a reasonable degree of liability limitation with respect to your members, an LLC is likely to be a good choice.

Forming an LLC starts with having a competent business attorney draft your Articles of Organization and your Operating Agreement. You should have an actual attorney draft these important document. Do not try to Do-It-Yourself (DIY), because you will not correctly draft these documents, and the mistakes you make can cost you more in the long run than it would cost you in the short term to have a competent business attorney do it correctly for you.

Getting your Articles of Organization and Operating Agreement from some website or "legal service" online is an equally poor choice, because such document dumps basically have the same relation to an actual law firm that the Salvation Army has to a retail store like Macy's. You're going to get something used that was designed for someone else or was designed to be a one-size-fits-all solution, but that does not actually meet your needs, because it was not designed specifically for your business with your business's unique legal concerns in mind. Perhaps worse, at some point in the future, if you have a problem, there is no one for you to hold accountable, and you are still likely to spend even more money on having an attorney untangle your DIY / template Articles of Organization and Operating Agreement than you would have spent having a competent business attorney draft them in the first place. Do a favor for Future You, and don't cut corners. Have a competent business attorney draft your Articles of Organization and Operating Agreement correctly the first time.

OTHER CONSIDERATIONS WHEN FORMING AN LLC

Every LLC will have an interest in establishing a strong trade name, often the most visible part of a business's brand aside from its logo. LLCs, like other business entities, can use trade names that do not include the names of the members. Registering your LLC's trade name with the Secretary of State in the state in which you do business may be necessary. In some states, like Tennessee, it is not necessary to register your LLC's trade name with the Secretary of State, but it may still be desirable to do so. You should consult a business attorney to help you make this decision.

You should also have your business attorney get an Employer Identification Number (EIN) from the Internal Revenue Service (I.R.S.) for your business. The LLC's members will want to use the EIN to open bank accounts and other accounts in the name of the business. Like any business, an LLC should maintain separate business accounts for operations, payroll, etc.

Having both an accountant and a business lawyer as part of your team are essential, even if you cannot afford to put either on your payroll. An attorney who serves as "general counsel" is the chief lawyer for a business; if that lawyer is independently contracted, and not on the business's payroll, he is said to be "outside general counsel" for the business. Outside general counsel services are crucial to a business's success, because legal services are necessary for every business,

and are one area where cutting corners will usually result in expensive problems later. Taking a proactive, preventive approach to your legal issues can seem costly, but the preventive approach is often far less expensive than the alternative –litigation. Obviously, unless you're a CPA, you also need an accountant for similar reasons. It's better to pay a little for bookkeeping services in advance than pay a lot when you get audited, later.

In addition to reiterating the need for having both outside general counsel and a CPA on your team, is the necessity of a written business plan. A business without a written business plan is like an ancient sailing ship on the high seas without a map. It might be a sunny day with wind in your sails when you start out, but a storm is coming, and you're going to get tossed around a bit. You better have a way to figure out where you are when that happens. A well-written, thorough business plan will keep you oriented on your priorities and help you stay on track, come what may.[17]

---

[17] See Chapter 10 for more information about business plans.

CHAPTER FOUR

CORPORATIONS

A corporation is a person. That might seem counter-intuitive, especially to people who believe corporations should not have certain rights and constitutional protections (e.g., freedom of speech, etc.) we normally extend to persons who are citizens of the U.S. This article will not discuss whether corporations should enjoy such rights; Citizens United has been decided, and the propriety of the outcome of that case is not the focus of this article. What we want to zero in on, here, is the essence of a corporation, and to really understand that, we need to acknowledge that, under current U.S. law, a corporation is a person.

Obviously, a corporation is not a natural person; so, how does it come to exist? The short answer is: an incorporator files the corporation's charter with the Secretary of State (and pays the related fee).

> "THE CHARTER IS THE DOCUMENT FILED TO BECOME INCORPORATED. IT IS COMPOSED OF THE ARTICLES OF INCORPORATION THAT SET FORTH CERTAIN MINIMUM INFORMATION ABOUT THE CORPORATION THAT IS REQUIRED BY LAW. THE INCORPORATOR IS THE PERSON THAT FILES THE CHARTER OF THE CORPORATION. THE INCORPORATOR MUST BE OF LEGAL AGE TO ENTER INTO CONTRACTS. ONCE THE ARTICLES OF INCORPORATION ARE FILED, THE INCORPORATOR'S FUNCTION IS COMPLETE."[18]

(This applies specifically to Tennessee corporations. Depending on your jurisdiction, your mileage may vary.) Once a corporation's charter has been filed and approved, it becomes incorporated. This is the birth of the corporation.

---

[18] TN Dept. of State, Business Services. (2014). Business Entity Filings FAQs. Retrieved January 2, 2020, from https://sos.tn.gov/products/business-services/business-entity-filings-faqs.

The corporation's charter defines the corporation's structure, hierarchy, and articulates much about how it will operate. What is not in the charter is often contained in the corporation's bylaws and other documents–for example, its Employee Handbook, etc. Every corporation is required by law to have at least one annual meeting, and corporations, generally speaking, are owned by one or more stockholders, and, therefore, they all issue one or more shares of stock in the corporation. This is a defining characteristic of corporations that sets it apart from partnerships (who have partners, not stockholders or members) and LLCs (who have members, not stockholders or partners). Often, Corporations also have either Executive Officers or Boards of Directors or both. Ultimately, the Executive Officers report to the Board of Directors and the Board of Directors usually reports to the shareholders. These are broad, general statements, but are true more often than not. Again, depending on the corporation and jurisdiction, your mileage may vary.

S-CORPORATIONS VS. C-CORPORATIONS

The default designation or status for a corporation is for it to be a "C-Corporation;" if the incorporator takes no specific action to specify the corporation as an "S-Corporation," it will be incorporated as a C-Corporation. Whichever form of corporation you choose, your corporation is entitled to limited liability, which is the primary reason most people incorporate. Beyond limited liability, people are familiar with the structure of a corporation–a separate legal entity ("person"), owned by shareholders, governed by a board of directors, the day-to-day operations of which are run by officers elected by that board.

Whether one chooses to file a one-page an "S-election" with the IRS or to remain a C-Corporation (by default) is largely a decision based on the preferred tax liability for the business. S-Corporations can be taxed almost like an LLC or Partnership. Corporations can switch between "S" and "C" status, but this decision should not be made lightly, as the tax ramifications of this decision are quite serious as we will discuss more, below.

Generally speaking, income from a corporation–specifically a C-Corporation–is taxed twice (three times, if you count Capital Gains Tax on the sale of shares of stock). The corporation first pays taxes on its net income. Then, shareholders pay tax, again, on distributions of profits (dividends, etc.). An S-Corporation can elect to be taxed only once, at the shareholder level, and, in this way, it is more similar to a partnership or a pass-through LLC for tax purposes.

WHY FORM A CORPORATION?

As mentioned, above, most people consider forming a corporation to obtain limited liability, to protect their personal assets from business risk, and to benefit from the corporate structure, the inherent benefits of which include a built-in system of checks and balances, among others. There is no limit to the number of shareholders a C-Corporation can have; S-Corporations, on the other hand, are limited to 100 shareholders who may only be U.S. citizens and resident aliens. Generally speaking, S-Corporations are also required to have only individual shareholders; and their fiscal year must track with the calendar year. Finally, if a corporation elects to be an S-Corporation, the only differences permitted between different classes of stock are differences in voting rights.

So, forming an S-Corporation is often preferable for small businesses, because the requirements with which an S-Corporation must comply force their tax reporting to track more closely with individual reporting than a C-Corporation's reporting forces it to do. Put another way, the S-Corporation's tax reporting is more likely to feel familiar to a small-business-person who may not be as sophisticated or may not have as many licensed professionals (accountants, attorneys, etc.) on staff to handle regulatory and tax compliance.

The above two paragraphs are really more properly described as "Why to consider an S-Corporation," rather than Why To Form a Corporation at all. In my opinion, if you are forming a corporation solely to limit your liability, you are likely making a hasty decision. For many small- or -medium-sized-businesses, an LLC will achieve an adequate liability limitation threshold at a lower operating cost than a corporation is likely to have. Choosing a corporation, in my opinion, should be done only when the corporate structure strongly appeals to the incorporator (or group of incorporators) and when the incorporator needs to raise large amounts of capital quickly.

OTHER CONSIDERATIONS WHEN FORMING A CORPORATION

An S-Corporation can be a good choice over an LLC, just as a C-Corporation can be a good choice over an S-Corporation. Each company, each incorporator (or organizer) must weigh a complex set of variables, costs, and benefits in choosing the type of entity to create, and that choice primarily should be based on the tax liabilities and the appeal (or lack thereof) of the business structure to the involved parties, which are going to have long-term impacts on the business's bottom line. If you are going to elect to form an S-Corporation, you should be aware that the accounting rules they are required to follow are complicated enough that converting from a C-Corporation to an S-Corporation can be difficult, and, therefore, expensive. For example, if an S-Corporation was a C-Corporation, and if it elected "S status" within the previous 10 years, it may face corporate tax (double taxation). Filing for S-Corporation election within 75 days of initially forming the corporation can enable you to avoid some of these complicated rules and reduce the cost of running your company; remember, you can always switch back to a C-Corporation, later.

Claiming business losses on his personal tax return might appeal to a small-business-person, and that's not possible with a C-Corporation, but it is possible with a pass-through S-Corporation. Also, the double taxation that attends C-Corporations can quickly wipe out profit margins for small businesses. However, these concerns—very real, very valid concerns—do not necessarily weigh in favor of the S-Corporation form for all incorporators.

Finally, every business—corporation, LLC, what-have-you is going to have a strong interest in establishing a powerful brand in their market. That is not inexpensive. So, when you invest in building your brand, you will want to protect it. That means having an attorney who can handle a broad spectrum of business legal issues, including intellectual property concerns. Corporations also have specific legal needs pertaining to securities regulation compliance.

Corporations absolutely must have legal counsel and an accountant. That does not mean they must hire an attorney and an accountant as employees, but a corporation that does not hire both an attorney and an accountant, at least, on a contract basis is taking an irresponsible risk about which its shareholders should be deeply concerned.

Having both an accountant and a business lawyer as part of your team are essential, even if you cannot afford to put either on your payroll. An attorney who serves as "general counsel" is the chief lawyer for a business; if that lawyer is independently contracted, and not on the business's payroll, he is said to be "outside general counsel" for the business. Outside general counsel services are crucial to a business's success, because legal services are necessary for every business, and are one area where cutting corners will usually result in expensive problems later. Taking a proactive, preventive approach to your legal issues can seem costly, but the preventive approach is often far less expensive than the alternative—litigation. Obviously, unless you're a CPA, you also need an accountant for similar reasons. It's better to pay a little for bookkeeping services in advance than pay a lot when you get audited, later.

In addition to reiterating the need for having both outside general counsel and a CPA on your team, is the necessity of a written business plan. A business without a written business plan is like an ancient sailing ship on the high seas without a map. It might be a sunny day with wind in your sails when you start out, but a storm is coming, and you're going to get tossed around a bit. You better have a way to figure out where you are when that happens. A well-written, thorough business plan will keep you oriented on your priorities and help you stay on track, come what may.

CHAPTER FIVE

DOING GOOD AND DOING WELL

Hopefully not later than 8th grade, you learned the difference between doing good and doing well. If you have lost focus on the distinction, recall that doing good has to do with adding to or enhancing positive aspects of life, whereas doing well generally refers to meeting with success, good health, and the like in one's life. This distinction is important to understand when asking the question, "Why should I form, or consider forming, a 501(c)(3) nonprofit organization?"

The answer, ultimately, is a bit complex, but, generally, comes down to whether your focus is on doing good or doing well. If your focus is on doing well, financially, you should not form a nonprofit, although you also might consider a social entrepreneurship business. If your focus is on doing good, however, a nonprofit organization might be a good vehicle for those efforts.

If you really want to do the most good, is a nonprofit really the way to go? Here's what LegalZoom® has to say about "Reasons to Form a Nonprofit Corporation":

AS SOMEONE INVOLVED WITH A CHARITABLE CAUSE, YOU MIGHT BE WEIGHING THE BENEFITS OF FORMALLY ORGANIZING YOUR NONPROFIT. WHILE IT MIGHT TAKE A LITTLE EXTRA WORK, ONLY WITH A STATE-RECOGNIZED NONPROFIT CORPORATION CAN YOU OBTAIN PRIVATE AND PUBLIC GRANTS, LOW-COST POSTAGE RATES AND BE EXEMPT FROM INCOME, SALES AND PROPERTY TAXES. MOST IMPORTANTLY, ONLY A FORMAL NONPROFIT CORPORATION ALLOWS INDIVIDUALS TO DONATE MONEY TAX-FREE, WHILE SHIELDING YOUR PERSONAL ASSETS FROM LIABILITY.[19]

---

[19] LegalZoom®. (2016, October 28). Reasons to Form a Nonprofit Corporation. Retrieved February 26, 2020, from https://www.legalzoom.com/knowledge/nonprofit/topic/reasons-to-form-non-profit

This is misleading, because the **benefits of** choosing to form a non-profit are different from the **reasons to** form a nonprofit. Describing the benefits of doing something is easier than making the case for actually doing that thing under a particular set of circumstances. While the benefits LegalZoom® has published on their website are technically accurate, with respect to nonprofit corporations, characterizing these benefits as reasons to form a nonprofit corporation is misleading.

The real reason to form a nonprofit organization is because one has met the following test:

1. One's focus is on doing good (i.e. achieving some goal which will add to, or enhance, some positive aspect of human life), rather than simply capturing revenue or redirecting financial resources;

2. One cannot more effectively and efficiently accomplish this goal through social entrepreneurship (i.e. a socially conscious, for-profit business enterprise);

3. No other nonprofit organization with a substantially similar mission exists; and

4. One has already built a team of potential advisors, volunteers, and leaders around a discrete mission statement and set of core values.

In all the years I have been practicing small business law, I have never encountered an entrepreneur or activist with an idea for a nonprofit that met this test.

Too often, when I ask someone why they want to start a nonprofit, they immediately start talking about getting grant money from the government. I think people like Matthew Lesko have done so much damage to our cultural perception of "money from the government" that a large number of people believe that the government is just giving money away for any old thing, and all they have to do is line up for a piece of the pie.

> "A 2004 report by the New York State Consumer Protection Board claimed that most of the grants mentioned in Lesko's books were actually public assistance programs that many people were not eligible for, and that Lesko misrepresented examples of people who had taken advantage of government programs.

The New York Times criticized him for having implied a current association with the paper long after ending a 1992–1994 *NYT* column.

In 2005, Lesko was named #99 in Bernard Goldberg's book *100 People Who Are Screwing Up America* because, 'He is a symbol for self-centered free-riders.'

In an interview with the *Washington Post* in July 2007, Lesko admitted having assembled his books from government guides to grants and loans, quoting Lesko as saying of his first book 'I plagiarized the whole thing' and 'I didn't write a lick.' Lesko later added "I get stuff for free and I sell it for as much as I can get.'"[20]

Lazy, narcissistic leeches are drawn to "free money from the government" because they feel entitled to be the recipients of money that was coercively taken from taxpayers, just because they think they have a good idea. Such is the extent of their hubris.

Good ideas are worthless; only execution on good ideas is valuable. If you have a truly valuable product or service, people will voluntarily pay you more for it than it costs you to produce and distribute it to them. Such voluntary exchanges the essence of free market capitalism. "Everything is worth what its purchaser will pay for it," said the first century B.C. Latin writer Publilius Syrus, and, nearly 2,100 years later, it's still true.

Even if your focus is in the right place (i.e. doing good), the odds are good that you can probably do good and do well through social entrepreneurship. If this is the case, you should pursue social entrepreneurship, because it is economically

---

[20] Wikimedia Foundation, Inc. (2020, January 21). Matthew Lesko. Retrieved February 26, 2020, from https://en.wikipedia.org/wiki/Matthew_Lesko#Criticism. See also: "How misleading advertising is feeding a nationwide boom in government grant scams" (PDF). New York State Consumer Protection Board. 2004. Archived from the original (PDF) on December 7, 2006. Retrieved 2006-04-30.; Fred, Joseph P. (3 March 2005). "Free Money? Sure. Heard of Food Stamps?". The New York Times. Retrieved 2006-04-22. "In August 2006, Lesko modified his credentials on his Web site, lesko.com, which described him (as his books did) as a columnist for Good Housekeeping Magazine and The New York Times Syndicate. He wrote the magazine column in the 1980s and the column for the syndicate from 1992 to 1994. Both organizations recently told him that these did not justify his suggestion of a current association."; Dhingra, Philip (8 Aug 2005). "Bernard Goldberg's 100 People Who Are Screwing Up America? And Why?". Philosophy History. "He is a symbol for self-centered free-riders"

productive (i.e. they produce wealth), whereas nonprofit activities are economically destructive (i.e. at best, they simply redistribute wealth, and create no new wealth).

If your focus is in the right place, and a nonprofit is actually the most efficient, effective way to do good, there probably is already a nonprofit organization the mission and values of which are substantially similar to the one you are considering creating. If this is the case, and it almost always is, then one would be better of collaborating with an existing nonprofit than competing with existing nonprofits for a finite pool of public and private funding.

Finally, assuming that your focus is in the right place, a nonprofit is actually the most efficient, effective way to do good, and there are no similar nonprofits out there, you'll need to build a strong team for your nonprofit organization to be able to do anything well. Initially, you'll need, at least, three people in key leadership roles—an executive (CEO), a treasurer (CFO), and an administrative / record-keeping professional (COO). You'll also need an accountant; a lawyer; an insurance agent; and volunteers and employees to handle everything your nonprofit will actually do to promote good in the world. Even small nonprofits are relatively expensive to create and operate, and the industry best practices guidelines for nonprofits restrict fundraising expenditures to 35% of the nonprofit's budget.[21] In both nonprofits and for profit companies, having the right teams in place makes the difference between success and failure. Don't start a nonprofit, and just assume that people will coalesce around your big idea. Start with the team; then, build the organization.

NONPROFITS VS. SOCIAL ENTREPRENEURSHIP

Unlike a nonprofit, social enterprises are for-profit businesses that also have a socially conscious purpose at the heart of their activities. In an LLC's well-written Operating Agreement, and in a corporation's well-written Charter, there is a statement describing the company's purpose. In a social enterprise, this statement of purpose will describe the social benefit the company is committed to pursuing, alongside a more common declaration that the company exists to engage in any legal, profitable activity.

---

[21] Give.Org BBB Wise Giving Alliance. (n.d.). Implementation Guide to the BBB Standards for Charity Accountability. Retrieved February 26, 2020, from http://www.give.org/for-charities/How-We-Accredit-Charities/implementation-guide/

There are two business organization structures designed to facilitate social entrepreneurship. These are low-profit limited liability companies (L3Cs) and benefit corporations. L3Cs cannot be organized in just any jurisdiction. Because LLCs, of all kinds, and corporations are created under the authority of a particular state, a state must enact a law that authorizes the creation of the relevant type of entity in that state. In other words, each state must have an L3C statute or a benefit corporation statute in order for such a company to be organized or incorporated in the state.

For example, Tennessee does not have an L3C statute, but Vermont, the first state to enact an L3C statute, still does. So, if one wants to operate an L3C in Tennessee, they should organize the company in a different jurisdiction, such as Vermont, and then apply for a Certificate of Authority to conduct business in Tennessee.

Keep in mind that, as a "foreign company" (i.e. a company organized outside of the State of Tennessee), an L3C will have additional regulatory compliance obligations and related expenses. In fact, this is one of the reasons, generally, why organizing or incorporating a company in one jurisdiction while operating it primarily outside that jurisdiction is not always efficient—especially for small businesses and start-ups. If one organizes an LLC in, say, Delaware or Nevada but they only really do business in Tennessee, or some other state, they have to pay for registration in both states. For a very small business, this often makes less sense than just organizing in the state where the business is primarily operated.

BENEFIT CORPORATIONS

"A BENEFIT CORPORATION IS A NEW LEGAL TOOL THAT CREATES A SOLID FOUNDATION FOR LONG TERM MISSION ALIGNMENT AND VALUE CREATION. IT PROTECTS MISSION THROUGH CAPITAL RAISES AND LEADERSHIP CHANGES, CREATES MORE FLEXIBILITY WHEN EVALUATING POTENTIAL SALE AND LIQUIDITY OPTIONS, AND PREPARES BUSINESSES TO LEAD A MISSION-DRIVEN LIFE POST-IPO.

A BENEFIT CORPORATION IS A TRADITIONAL CORPORATION WITH MODIFIED OBLIGATIONS COMMITTING IT TO HIGHER STANDARDS OF PURPOSE, ACCOUNTABILITY AND TRANSPARENCY:

1. PURPOSE: BENEFIT CORPORATIONS COMMIT TO CREATING PUBLIC BENEFIT AND SUSTAINABLE VALUE IN ADDITION TO GENERATING PROFIT. THIS SUSTAINABILITY IS AN INTEGRAL PART OF THEIR VALUE PROPOSITION.

2. ACCOUNTABILITY: BENEFIT CORPORATIONS ARE COMMITTED TO CONSIDERING THE COMPANY'S IMPACT ON SOCIETY AND THE ENVIRONMENT IN ORDER TO CREATE LONG-TERM SUSTAINABLE VALUE FOR ALL STAKEHOLDERS.

3. TRANSPARENCY: BENEFIT CORPORATIONS ARE REQUIRED TO REPORT, IN MOST STATES ANNUALLY AND USING A THIRD PARTY STANDARD, SHOWING THEIR PROGRESS TOWARDS ACHIEVING SOCIAL AND ENVIRONMENTAL IMPACT TO THEIR SHAREHOLDERS AND IN MOST CASES THE WIDER PUBLIC.

TRADITIONAL CORPORATIONS ARE EXPECTED TO USE PROFIT MAXIMIZATION AS THE PRIMARY LENS IN DECISION MAKING. MANY NOW SEE THIS AS A HURDLE IN CREATING LONG-TERM VALUE FOR ALL STAKEHOLDERS, INCLUDING THE SHAREHOLDERS THEMSELVES. BENEFIT CORPORATIONS REJECT THIS MYOPIC MODEL. THEY ARE REQUIRED TO CONSIDER ALL STAKEHOLDERS IN THEIR DECISIONS. THIS GIVES THEM THE FLEXIBILITY TO CREATE LONG TERM VALUE FOR ALL STAKEHOLDERS OVER THE LONG TERM, AND EVEN THROUGH EXIT TRANSACTIONS SUCH AS IPOS AND ACQUISITIONS."[22]

Benefit corporations can be incorporated in 36 states (another 5 are currently working on benefit corporation legislation), as of the time of this writing. While I tend to recommend L3Cs over benefit corporations, in general, this has more to do with a preference for limited liability companies over corporations, in general, than it does with the social entrepreneurship aspects of either business structure.

---

[22] B Lab. (2020). Benefit Corporation. Retrieved March 6, 2020, from https://benefitcorp.net/what-is-a-benefit-corporation

LOW-PROFIT LIMITED LIABILITY COMPANIES (L³CS)

This section builds on the information on L³Cs in Chapter Three.[23] If it's been a while since you read that section, you should go back and review it, now.

STATE-SPECIFIC L³C LAWS

Only a few states currently have L³C statutes permitting their organization in the relevant jurisdictions. These states sometimes have very specific laws pertaining to how L³Cs must be operated, at a corporate level. Below are a few examples, but this is not intended to be a comprehensive list.

Indiana:

At all times, L³Cs must significantly further accomplishment of one or more charitable or educational purposes, and must not have been formed but for the company's relationship to the accomplishment of such charitable or educational purposes. The intention to qualify as an L³C shall be indicated in the company's Articles of Organization.[24]

Louisiana:

L³Cs must set forth, in their Articles of Organization, that they have the purpose of significantly furthering one or more charitable or educational causes. Further, they may have no significant purpose related to the production of income or property appreciation; and they may have no significant political or legislative purpose.[25]

Maine:

At all times, L³Cs must significantly further the accomplishment of one or more charitable or educational purposes, and will not qualify as a low-profit LLC, but

---

[23] See the last few paragraphs of the "LLC Taxonomy" section of Chapter Three.

[24] 805 ILCS 180/1-26.

[25] La. Rev. Stat. Ann. § 12:1302

for their relationship to the accomplishment of such charitable or educational purposes.[26]

Michigan:

The names of L3Cs must contain the words "low-profit limited liability company" or the abbreviation "L.3.C." or "l.3.c." with or without periods or other punctuation.[27]

In their Articles of Organization, L3Cs must include the one or more charitable or education purposes that they exist to address, and, at all times, must conduct activities that further such purposes. Further, they may have no significant purpose regarding the production of income or property appreciation, and may have no significant political or legislative purpose. Mich. Comp. Laws Serv. § 450.4102.

Rhode Island:

At all times, L3Cs must significantly further the accomplishment of one or more charitable or education purposes, and must not have been formed but for the company's relationship to the accomplishment of charitable or educational purposes.[28]

Utah:

In its Articles of Organization, each L3C must state (1) that it is a low-profit limited liability company, and (2) that its business purpose is to significantly further the accomplishment of one or more charitable or education purposes. Additionally, an L3C is a company that would not have been formed but for its relationship to, or accomplishment of, charitable or educational purposes. No L3C may have a significant purpose related to the production of income or property appreciation; and no L3C may have a significant political or legislative purpose.[29]

---

[26] Me. Rev. Stat. tit. 31, § 1611.

[27] Mich. Comp. Laws Serv. § 450.4204.

[28] R.I. Gen. Laws § 7-16-76.

[29] Utah Code Ann. § 48-3a-1302.

Vermont: ⭐

L³Cs must significantly further the accomplishment of one or more charitable or education purposes, may not be a company that would have been formed but for its relationship to accomplishment of charitable/educational purposes, and can have no significant purpose to produce income or capital appreciation of property. Finally, no L³C may have a purpose to accomplish one or more political or legislative purposes.[30]

Wyoming:

In its Articles of Organization, each L³C must state that it furthers the accomplishment of one or more charitable or education purposes; that it would not have been formed but for its relationship to said purposes; that it has no significant purpose to produce income or capital appreciation of property; and that it has no significant purpose to pursue the accomplishment of political or legislative purposes.[31]

L³C AVAILABILITY

As of the time of this writing, only about eight (8) states have L³C statutes. Consulting with an attorney, *before* organizing an L³C (or benefit corporation) and *before* engaging in social enterprise efforts is especially important. Complying with the regulations that particularly and uniquely apply to L³Cs can be relatively complex, especially when dealing with matters relating to state-level taxation in states that have no L³C statute.

In Tennessee's 108th General Assembly2013-2014, State Senator John Stevens (R) introduced SB 506.[32] This bill would have authorized "the creation of a new type of limited liability company, in Tennessee, the low-profit limited liability company ("L³C")." Under the legal paradigm which would have been created, had the proposed bill been signed into law, an...

---

[30] Vt. Stat. Ann. tit. 11, § 4162. (Vermont gets the Gold Star, because it was first to pass an L³C statute, and continues to be a great jurisdiction in which to operate an L³C.)

[31] Wyo. Stat. § 17-29-102.

[32] HB 497 concurrently introduced by Representative Sanderson.

"L3C [WOULD BE] AN LLC FORMED FOR A BUSINESS PURPOSE THAT SATISFIES THE FOLLOWING REQUIREMENTS:

(1) SIGNIFICANTLY FURTHERS THE ACCOMPLISHMENT OF MAKING CONTRIBUTIONS FOR CHARITABLE OR EDUCATIONAL PURPOSES;

(2) WOULD NOT HAVE BEEN FORMED BUT FOR THE COMPANY'S RELATIONSHIP TO THE ACCOMPLISHMENT OF CHARITABLE OR EDUCATIONAL PURPOSES;

(3) NO SIGNIFICANT PURPOSE OF THE LLC IS THE PRODUCTION OF INCOME OR THE APPRECIATION OF PROPERTY; PROVIDED, HOWEVER, THAT THE LONE FACT THAT AN LLC PRODUCES SIGNIFICANT INCOME OR CAPITAL APPRECIATION WILL NOT BE CONCLUSIVE EVIDENCE OF A SIGNIFICANT PURPOSE INVOLVING THE PRODUCTION OF INCOME OR THE APPRECIATION OF PROPERTY; AND

(4) NO PURPOSE OF THE COMPANY IS TO ACCOMPLISH POLITICAL OR LEGISLATIVE PURPOSES."[33]

SB 506 was introduced on the 31st of January, 2013, was passed on first consideration, was passed on second consideration, and was referred to the Senate's Commerce & Labor Committee.[34] The house passed its companion bill, HB 497, on first consideration; and, upon passing on second consideration, referred it to the Business and Utilities Committee–Government Operations, for review. On the 5th of February, 2013, it was assigned to the Business and Utilities Subcommittee. Each of these bills died in committee, having never been

[33] Tennessee General Assembly. (2014). SB0506 Bill Summary. Retrieved March 20, 2020, from http://wapp.capitol.tn.gov/apps/Billinfo/default.aspx?BillNumber=SB0506&ga=108

[34] For more information on the legislative process, and how a bill becomes a law, in Tennessee, see Tennessee General Assembly. (2020). How a Bill Becomes a Law. Retrieved March 20, 2020, from http://www.capitol.tn.gov/about/billtolaw.html

reported out of these committees or recommended out of the committees for passage.

Because Tennessee has never passed a law authorizing the creation of an L3C in the state, L3Cs may not be organized in Tennessee, under Tennessee law. Under federal law, however, each state must give full faith and credit to the laws of each other state.

> "FULL FAITH AND CREDIT SHALL BE GIVEN IN EACH STATE TO THE PUBLIC ACTS, RECORDS, AND JUDICIAL PROCEEDINGS OF EVERY OTHER STATE. AND THE CONGRESS MAY BY GENERAL LAWS PRESCRIBE THE MANNER IN WHICH SUCH ACTS, RECORDS AND PROCEEDINGS SHALL BE PROVED, AND THE EFFECT THEREOF."[35]

Despite this powerful and important feature of Constitutional Law, nothing in Constitution insures unlimited extraterritorial recognition of all statutes or of any statute under all circumstances.[36] So, in the absence of a law that *prohibits* the recognition of the L3C structure in a state, or otherwise governs how a foreign L3C will be treated by a state without an L3C statute, foreign L3Cs operate in a kind-of grey area, but tend to be able to receive the same kinds of recognition a regular LLC would receive.

Therefore, if one organized an L3C in a state, such as Vermont, the L3C could conduct business, as a foreign LLC, in Tennessee. "Before transacting business in [Tennessee], a foreign LLC shall obtain a certificate of authority."[37] At the time of this writing, one may obtain a copy of the Application for Certificate of Authority (LLC), Form SS-4233, from the Office of the Secretary of State of Tennessee, or said office's website.[38]

---

[35] USCS Const. Art. IV § 1.

[36] *Yellow Cab Transit Co. v. Overcash*, 133 F.2d 228 (8th Cir. 1942).

[37] T.C.A. § 48-249-904.

[38] https://sos.tn.gov/products/business-services/application-certificate-authority-ss-4233

Form SS-4233 comes with relatively extensive instructions, and provides, in a dedicated section regarding filing fees:

"THE FILING FEE FOR APPLICATION FOR CERTIFICATE OF AUTHORITY IS $50.00 PER MEMBER IN EXISTENCE ON THE DATE OF THE FILING, WITH A MINIMUM FEE OF $300.00 AND A MAXIMUM FEE OF $3,000."

"PURSUANT TO T.C.A. § 48-249-913(D), ADDITIONAL FILING FEES MAY APPLY IF THE LLC COMMENCED DOING BUSINESS IN TENNESSEE PRIOR TO THE APPROVAL OF THE APPLICATION. IF A PRIOR DATE IS INDICATED IN SECTION 2 [OF FORM SS-4233], A CALL TO THE BUSINESS SERVICES DIVISION CUSTOMER SERVICE LINE AT (615) 741-2286 IS ENCOURAGED FOR GUIDANCE ON THE APPROPRIATE FILING FEE AMOUNT."

This is a good opportunity to note, regarding forming LLCs in other states and operating them in states other than the one in which they are domiciled, that filing fees for registration in states, in which the foreign LLC is transacting business, can quickly accumulate. In Tennessee, the filing fee for Form SS-4233 is the same as the filing fee for Articles of Organization. Creating a foreign LLC and transacting business in Tennessee will result in the same costs (in Tennessee) as just creating a domestic LLC, *plus* the costs of maintaining the state's domicile in a foreign jurisdiction. For this reason, I tend to recommend that, unless one needs a form of LLC not available in Tennessee, such as an L3C, they're better off just forming the LLC in Tennessee if they plan to primarily (or exclusively) transact business within the state. Usually, this recommendation is provided in response to a question about whether or not its best to organize the LLC in Delaware, Nevada, Wyoming, etc.

Fortunately, Tennessee has no income tax. In a state like Alabama, however, an L3C will be well-advised to obtain tax planning services from a business tax attorney, because the L3C and/or its members will be subject to both state and federal income taxes. Like any other limited liability company, L3Cs can be disregarded entities (i.e. taxed like a sole proprietorship or partnership), but one's business tax attorney should pay special attention to the differences in the way a state that has no L3C statute, for tax purposes, may treat L3Cs differently from regular LLCs.

UNDERSTANDING PROGRAM-RELATED INVESTMENTS (PRIS)

The primary benefit of an L3C is its potential for strategic partnerships with 501(c)(3) non-profit companies or private foundations. The cornerstone of these partnerships are Program-related Investments, or "PRIs".[39]

A PRI is an investment "in which:

1. The primary purpose is to accomplish one or more of the foundation's[40] exempt purposes,

2. Production of income or appreciation of property is not a significant purpose, and

3. Influencing legislation or taking part in political campaigns on behalf of candidates is not a purpose." *Id.*

You'll recall, from the above discussion on state-specific L3C laws, these are all key features of L3Cs. This is an extreme over-simplification, but non-profits, essentially, can make narrowly-tailored investments in L3Cs, which, *technically*, are for-profit legal entities. These investments could generate a positive return on investment (ROI) for the non-profits. The practical upshot of this, of course, is that non-profits could use smart investments, in lieu of traditional fundraising, to generate the revenue they need.

In short, PRIs are (1) funding opportunities to which L3Cs have access, but traditional LLCs will not; and (2) opportunities for non-profits to receive a return on invested capital, rather than relying entirely on grants and traditional fundraising activities. PRIs align the incentives of non-profits and L3Cs, bringing them into a harmonious balance, and making them each better off for their collaborative efforts.

It's a shame more states haven't recognized the value of L3Cs, and adopted L3C statutes. Still, if social entrepreneurship is your passion, you can form an L3C in one state and operate it, as a limited liability company, in another.

------

[39] U.S. Treasury, IRS. (2020, February 13). Program-Related Investments. Retrieved March 30, 2020, from https://www.irs.gov/charities-non-profits/private-foundations/program-related-investments

[40] Here, it's just as good to read "non-profit," I believe.

CHAPTER SIX

MAKING THE RIGHT CHOICE FOR YOUR BUSINESS

There is no magic pill, no silver bullet, no "right answer," no one-size-fits all solution that will work for every business. There is no formula to follow to guarantee that your business is structured correctly. In business, as in life, there are no guarantees. The good news, however, is that if you have read and understood the contents of this paper and consulted a business attorney, and if you know your business well (i.e., you have a well-crafted, written business plan), you probably have enough information to confidently make the right choice of business organization to fit your company's needs.

Don't worry if you choose—or *have chosen*—poorly. You can always change the organizational structure and of your business. There are costs involved (there is no such thing as a free lunch), but the costs are manageable.

Most people have the wrong frame of mind, when they approach the question, "Which business organization (i.e. structure) is right for my business?" The mistake most people make is to reduce the scope of their consideration to one or two simple factors. They primarily consider either legal risk or tax implications, or both. Rarely do they think about much else when choosing between LLC, corporation, partnership, or any of their other options. Many small business owners just skip the question, altogether, and, consequently, end up in either a sole proprietorship or general partnership.

Avoiding thinking about the question, or being too reductive in doing so, is the wrong approach. So, what's the right approach?

The right approach to deciding which business organization is right for your business begins with the right frame of mind, or "mindset." Take a holistic approach. Think about every part of your business. Ask yourself, how will being an LLC, partnership, corporation, or sole proprietorship affect each part of *what I do* and *the business of what I do*. Remember, those are two separate things.

What you do is sell goods or services. The *business of what you do* is the work of creating and managing the business organization that sells the goods or services.

When most entrepreneurs think about "running the business," they tend to think about the day-to-day selling of goods or services. Whether the business is an LLC or a corporation, a sole proprietorship, or a partnership, someone has to show up, do the work, make the customers or clients or patients happy, and count the money.

Consider, however, that your business's relationships with every single person with whom, or legal entity with which, it conducts business has legal rights which may be affected by your business's organization. Let's look a typical example:

If you're running a small, family restaurant, and you ask your seafood supplier to let you pay for your fish and the like on NET 60 terms, rather than NET 30 terms, whether your business is a General Partnership, LP, LLP, or LLC will make a difference. If your business is a General Partnership, the seafood supplier can collect up to 100% of any balance owed on your account from any of the partners. If your business is an LP, they'll only be able to collect 100% if they can collect from the General Partner or all the partners, together. If your business is an LLP, they can they'll only be able to collect 100% if they can collect from all the partners, together. If it's an LLC, they're going to need a personal guaranty, or they'll be running the risk that, if the business defaults on its obligation to pay, they're going to be unable to collect against anything but the business's assets—which might be worthless or nonexistent.

Whether customers, vendors, suppliers, or others can sue the people who run a business often depends on both the type of business organization and the cause of action. If a person commits fraud, for example, their LLC or corporation will not protect them, because a Court may elect to <u>pierce the corporate veil</u>. The incentives that arise as a direct or indirect result of the way a business is organized will have ripple effects throughout all the systems and processes the business develops and implements.

As further discussed in Chapter Ten, you should write a business plan for your business. This is not a one-time exercise. It's something you'll need to revisit from time to time, as your business evolves, adding to it, removing things that don't work, and using it to keep your business on track with the goals you've had from the beginning. When you're thinking through the important question of how to structure your business, you should consider things like:

• The frequency with which you'll need to raise capital, whether through debt or equity investment in the business;

- The nature of the relationships between those who work for your business and the business, *per se;*

  - Are they employees or independent contractors?

  - What, if any, exposure does your business have with respect to your workers?

  - How likely is it that, in the event of a lawsuit, the business's owners or operators would be sued, if the business is not an LLC or corporation—and does it really matter, under the circumstances?); and

  - Many other questions like these will arise, and need to be addressed;

- What about vendors and suppliers? How will your organization adjust their incentives?

- How will your business organization choice adjust the incentives of the owners of the business?

- How will your business organization choice adjust the incentives of the officers of the business, assuming some officers are not owners?

- How will your business organization choice adjust your customers', clients', or patients' incentives?

Incentives matter.[41] Whether or not they realize it, your decision to structure your business one way or another—to choose one business organization over another—will have a profound impact on the incentives of each person who, or legal entity that, interacts with your business.

It's your job, as an entrepreneur, or business decision-maker, to ensure that your business organization is optimized for the way you do your business. This means taking a holistic look at the who, what, when, where, why, and how of your business—not just one dimension of your business's life, such as taxation or legal liability. Being a single-issue voter is a lazy, stupid approach to politics, and making this important decision based on a single issue is, likewise, lazy and stupid. You can be better than that, and a good business lawyer can help.

---

[41] Gwartney, J. D., Stroup, R. L., Lee, D. R., Ferrarini, T. H., & Calhoun, J. (2016). *Common Sense Economics: What Everyone Should Know about Wealth and Prosperity* (3rd ed.). New York: St. Martins Press.

CHAPTER SEVEN

A BRIEF OVERVIEW OF INTELLECTUAL PROPERTY

Protecting your brand and other Intellectual Property ("IP") almost always involves enlisting the aid of an attorney who can handle intellectual property concerns. So, before you do anything discussed in this chapter, get yourself an IP lawyer, and discuss with them what IP you have. This chapter is meant to help establish a foundation for that conversation.

IP OVERVIEW: THE KINDS OF IP

1. **Patents**. "A patent is a limited duration property right relating to an invention, granted by the United States Patent and Trademark Office in exchange for public disclosure of the invention."[42]

2. **Copyrights**. Copyright protection subsists, in accordance with this title, in original works of authorship fixed in any tangible medium of expression, now known or later developed, from which they can be perceived, reproduced, or otherwise communicated, either directly or with the aid of a machine or device. Works of authorship include the following categories:

   a. Literary works;

   b. Musical works, including any accompanying words;

   c. Dramatic works, including any accompanying music;

   d. Pantomimes and choreographic works;

---

[42] U.S. Patent and Trademark Office. "Patent FAQs." United States Patent and Trademark Office - An Agency of the Department of Commerce, 13 Dec. 2019, www.uspto.gov/help/patent-help.

e. Pictorial, graphic, and sculptural works;

   f. Motion pictures and other audiovisual works;

   g. Sound recordings; and

   h. Architectural works.

   In no case, however, does copyright protection for an original work of authorship extend to any idea, procedure, process, system, method of operation, concept, principle, or discovery, regardless of the form in which it is described, explained, illustrated, or embodied in such work.

   In other words, a copyright protects each expression of an idea, not the idea, *per se*.

3. **Trademarks**. Trade marks and service marks—collectively and colloquially referred to as "trademarks"—are marks that indicate the source of goods or services. These marks include word marks, such as trade names and slogans; logos; and composite marks, which combine a word or words and a design or designs.

4. **Trade Secrets**. To qualify for trade secret protection, a purported trade secret must:

   a. Consist of the type of information that is protectable as a trade secret (the "eligible subject matter requirement");

   b. Be secret ("actual secrecy requirement");

   c. Derive actual or potential independent economic value from not being generally known to or readily ascertainable through proper means by another person who could obtain economic value from the disclosure or use of the information ("independent economic value requirement"); and

   d. Have been the subject of efforts reasonable under the circumstances to protect its secrecy ("reasonable efforts requirement").

PATENTS

A patent provides the exclusive right, for a specified number of years, to utilize a clearly defined invention or, if that right is assigned to another person or entity, the right to collect royalties on the utilization of the invention.

U.S. patent documents often include drawings, diagrams, or both. The patent document describes the invention, and concludes with a section called "claims." The claims describe the limits of the patent owner's exclusive rights.

In the United States, patent applications are processed, and patents are granted, by the U.S. Patent and Trademark Office (USPTO). The USPTO is a federal government agency, and is a part of the U.S. Department of Commerce. In the U.S., individual states do not have the legal authority to grant patents, and patents exclusively are governed by federal law. Unlike other types of intellectual property rights, such as trademarks, copyright, and trade secrets, patent right do not exist until the government grants the patent.

If you have IP you believe qualifies for a patent, you should contact a patent attorney, and use their services to secure your legal rights in your IP. Under no circumstances should you attempt to DIY your legal work, in general, and that is especially true of highly specialized legal work, such as applying for or defending patents.

COPYRIGHTS

Copyrights spring into existence the moment a creative work is created. Subject matter eligible for copyright protection ("copyright-eligible subject matter") is entitled to legal copyright protection if it is both "original" and fixed in a "tangible medium of expression." Technically, neither registration nor use of a copyright notice is strictly required for copyright protection. Nevertheless, both are beneficial.

What does it mean to be "original," when nearly every creative endeavor is, to some degree, derivative? Under copyright law, original work is independently created by the author and merely possesses "some minimal degree of creativity."[43] Original, in this sense, is not synonymous with "novel," as the latter term is employed in U.S. patent law. Therefore, a work of authorship may be

---

[43] *Feist Publications, Inc. v. Rural Tel. Servs. Co.*, 499 U.S. 340 (1991).

entitled to copyright protection, even if it is not entirely new or hitherto unimagined.

The creativity requirement distinguishes copyrightable works of authorship from simple recitations of facts, or some other work completely devoid of creativity. Note, however, that the degree of creativity required is *minimal*. Even if a work has only an iota of creativity, it will meet the creativity requirement, even if it is "crude, humble or obvious." *Id*.

Typically, the author of copyright-eligible subject matter owns the copyright. An exception to this general rule, however, is a "work made for hire." When an employee, in the scope of their employment, creates copyright-eligible subject matter, their employer is presumed to be the author and, thus, is the legal owner of the copyright.[44] Such works are referred to as works made for hire. Individuals and legal entities can alter this default rule by using a contract.

Works created by an independent contractor (i.e. commissioned works) are not legally deemed to be works made for hire unless the parties otherwise expressly agree in writing that they are, and the work fits into one of the statutory categories in 17 U.S.C. § 101:

- A contribution to a collective work

- A portion of a motion picture or other audiovisual work

- A translation

- A supplementary work[45]

- A compilation

- An instructional text

- A test

- An answer material for a test; or

- An atlas.

Outside one of these categories, commissioned works do not qualify as works made for hire. Even so, the person commissioning the author may obtain the copyright in a commissioned work by obtaining a written assignment of the copyright from the independent contractor.

One must sue for copyright infringement lawsuit in federal court, if at all. A prerequisite to filing such a suit is registration of the copyright. Registration does not occur "when an application for registration is filed, but when the [Register of Copyrights] has registered a copyright after examining a properly filed

---

[44] 17 U.S.C. § 101.

[45] A work created in order to introduce, explain, revise, etc. another author's work.

application."[46] When a copyright owner needs to reduce the delay otherwise resulting when seeking registration, he may request "special handling" (for a fee) from the Copyright Office. Typically, typically a request for special handling will be granted in consideration of prospective litigation. If granted, special handling reduces the wait time for registration to five (5) days.

Copyright notices are not mandatory for works published on or after the 1st of March, 1989. Nevertheless, the Copyright Act does provide authors an incentive for affixing to their works a copyright notice. Specifically, if a work bears proper notice, defendants are not permitted to rely on the defense of "innocent infringement" (i.e. "I didn't know it wasn't copyright-eligible subject matter") in order to mitigate actual damages or statutory damages in a copyright infringement lawsuit.[47]

The prevailing party in a copyright lawsuit may be entitled to attorney's fees, depending on a variety of factors. Before filing a copyright lawsuit, one should discuss with their attorney the likelihood of recovering damages, including attorney's fees.

TRADEMARKS

Typically, trademarks are designs, phrases, symbols, or words used as to identify the source of goods. Service marks are identical to trademarks, except their use exclusively pertains to services rather than physical products or "goods". Colloquially, however, trademarks and service marks are both referred to as "trademarks" or "marks."

Trade names and logos are what most people think of, first, when they think about trademarks, but there are other materials that have the potential to be eligible for protection as a trademark. These include characters (Bugs Bunny), colors (T-Mobile Magenta), product packaging, also known as "trade dress" (think bottle shapes for Heinz tomato ketchup, Coca-Cola soft drinks, A1 steak sauce, etc.), slogans (Apple – "Think Different"), and sounds (MGM's roaring lion). Using something to designate the source of the goods or services is a prerequisite to considering that thing a trademark. Anything merely functional, generic, or ornamental will be disqualified for trademark protection.

---

[46] *Fourth Estate Pub. Ben. Corp. v. Wall-Street.com, LLC*, 139 S. Ct. 881 (Mar. 4, 2019).

[47] 17 U.S.C. § 401(d).

The purpose of legally protecting owners' interests in their trademarks to protect consumers inauthentic providers of specific goods and services who are simply copying authentic providers of the same. Additionally, trademarks protect protect trademark owners' goodwill and reputation. Without trademark law, consumers would struggle to identify and differentiate between brands. Preventing unauthorized parties from using trademarks they do not own, confusingly similar marks, gives consumers confidence in the consistency of quality and features of the products or services offered in connection with certain marks. Because, trademark law's basic aim is to reduce the likelihood of consumer confusion in the marketplace, that is the fundamental issue of any trademark claim—whether or not one person's use of a trademark is likely to cause confusion for a reasonable consumer in the market for the related goods or services.

Trademark owners have exclusive control over the use of their trademarks, subject to various limitations, including:
- Acquiescence,
- The Fair Use Doctrine,
- The First Sale Doctrine, and
- Laches.

These limitations are beyond the scope of this book, but you should discuss them with your general counsel (or IP attorney).

Trademarks can be registered at both the state and federal levels, and state registration is far less expensive, but illustrates the old adage: "You get what you pay for." At the federal level, the scope of one's trademark protection is far more extensive than at the state level.

If one must sue a person for trademark infringement or dilution, what award from the Court's judgment can the winner of such a lawsuit expect to receive? First, and most commonly, one may receive an injunction (also called "equitable relief"), whereby the Court orders a person to do, or refrain from doing, a specific action. Prohibitory injunctions require one to stop doing certain acts (e.g. selling products bearing infringing trademarks). Mandatory, or affirmative, injunctions require one to do take specific acts, such as:
- Destroying, selling, or turning over to the other party, all products bearing the infringing mark(s);
- Disclaiming—on packaging, marketing materials, the internet, etc.—any affiliation with the other party;
- Modifying its trademark; or
- Running advertising suitable to correct the confusion caused by infringement.

Secondly, the Court may award monetary damages. As alluded to, above, injunctive relief is the most common remedy awarded in a trademark infringement action. Nevertheless, Section 1117(a) of the Lanham Act allows a successful plaintiff to recover monetary damages for trademark infringement and false designation of origin claims. These monetary damages can include:

- Actual damages;

- Defendant's profits; and

- Costs (including, but not limited to, attorneys' fees).[48]

Under the Lanham Act, Plaintiffs are not entitled to punitive damages, but may be entitled to recover such damages under one or more state law unfair competition claims.[49]

In their discretion, Courts may also increase actual damages up to triple the amount awarded (treble damages). In their discretion, Courts may increase or decrease—by any amount—an award of profits, if the Court holds that a recovery of actual profits is "either inadequate or excessive."[50] An enhancement of damages almost always follows a Court's finding of willful infringement, but enhancements of damages are not permitted to be punitive.[51]

TRADE SECRETS

Trade secrets are governed by both federal law and the laws of the various states. Before the nearly ubiquitous adoption of the Uniform Trade Secret Act (UTSA), courts relied heavily upon the Restatement of Torts. The Restatement of Torts states the various factors a Court should consider when determining whether certain information qualifies as a legally protectable trade secret. The Restatement of Torts also describes the circumstances under which one's unauthorized disclosure, or one's use of another's, trade secret gives rise to an action for trade secret misappropriation. In trade secret cases, Courts in every state continue to on guidance from the Restatement of Torts. In recent years, however, statutes, such as the UTSA (as adopted and amended by the various

---

[48] 15 U.S.C. § 1117(a).

[49] See, for example, *Duncan v. Stuetzle*, 76 F.3d 1480 (9th Cir. 1996).

[50] 15 U.S.C. 1117(a)(3).

[51] *Playboy Enterprises, Inc. v. P.K. Sorren Export Co.*, 546 F. Supp. 987, 998 (S.D. Fla. 1982); 15 U.S.C. 1117(a).

states) and the federal Defend Trade Secrets Act, have come to be the primary basis for most trade secret suits.

In the 1980s, various states began adopting and amending the UTSA. The UTSA, defines misappropriation and the proper subject matter for trade secret protection, just as the Restatement of Torts did. The UTSA goes further, however, and provides for:

- Preemption of other misappropriation causes of action (excluding contract claims arising from trade secret misappropriation);

- Preservation of secrecy in litigation;

- Remedies for misappropriation;

- Statutes of limitations; and

- More uniform application of the law amongst states.

As of 2020, 48 states, the District of Columbia, Puerto Rico, and the U.S. Virgin Islands have adopted the UTSA or a statute closely based on it. New York, continuing to rely on the Restatement of Torts, and North Carolina, which has a trade secret statute not based on the UTSA, are the only two states that do not use the UTSA.

The Defend Trade Secrets Act (DTSA) was enacted on, and became effective as of, the 11th of May, 2016. The DTSA provides a federal, private cause of action for trade secret misappropriation.[52] The key definitions of the DTSA are taken from the UTSA. Therefore, pleading and evidence requirements to establish a claim for trade secret misappropriation are the same under both laws.

The three key differences between the two acts have to do with jurisdiction, scope of applicability, and equitable remedies. Unlike the UTSA, the DTSA:

- Gives federal courts original jurisdiction over all trade secret claims that are brought under the DTSA;[53]

- Is limited to trade secret claims "related to a product or service used in, or intended for use in, interstate or foreign commerce," and, therefore, doesn't apply to trade secrets exclusively used in, or intended for use in, intrastate commerce;[54] and

---

[52] 18 U.S.C. § 1833(b)(1).

[53] 18 U.S.C. § 1836(c).

[54] 18 U.S.C. § 1836(b)(1).

- Under "extraordinary circumstances" and when necessary to prevent the dissemination of a misappropriated trade secret, provides for *ex parte* seizures of property for example, where a defendant might flee the country or immediately disclose the trade secret to a third party.[55]

The DTSA does not preempt state trade secret law, in general. Nevertheless, under federal and state law, the DTSA practically immunizes individuals from liability for certain confidential disclosures of trade secrets.[56] Such immunity is an affirmative defense; therefore, a defendant has the burden of establishing an entitlement to the immunity.[57]

Under the DTSA, in any contract or agreement with an "employee" (which is defined to include traditional employees, independent contractors, and consultants), employers must provide notice of the Act's immunities from disclosure concerning the use of a trade secret or other confidential information.[58] This notice requirement only applies to contracts and agreements entered into after DTSA went into effect.[59] Failure to comply does not impact state law trade secret claims. Under the DTSA, failure to comply with this notice requirement only bars the recovery of *exemplary* damages or attorneys' fees against an employee who did not received a required notice.[60]

There are other federal trade secret laws and regulations that can provide limited protection of trade secrets, too. Each of these are quite specific in their "use cases," and one would be well-advised not to try to shoehorn the use of one of these laws outside their intended purpose.

The Economic Espionage Act (EEA), which provides criminal and civil sanctions for the misappropriation of a trade secret benefitting a foreign government, is also probably not going to impact too many small businesses or start-ups. Also, note that the EEA deals primarily with the *penalties* for *misappropriation*, which is already illegal under the DTSA, UTSA, et al.

---

[55] 18 U.S.C. § 1836(b)(2)(A).

[56] 18 U.S.C. § 1833(b).

[57] *Unum Grp. v. Loftus*, 220 F. Supp. 3d 143 (D. Mass. 2016).

[58] 18 U.S.C. § 1833(b)(3)(A).

[59] 18 U.S.C. § 1833(b)(3)(D).

[60] 18 U.S.C. § 1833(b)(3)(C).

The Freedom of Information Act (FoIA or "FOIA," often read as "foi-ya" or "foïa"), which includes a provision that exempts trade secret information from disclosure, can sometimes be used to access information the government is otherwise reluctant or unwilling to disclose. One will not be able to use a FOIA request to access trade secrets, however, as they are exempt.

The federal Trade Secret Act (TSA), which prohibits the unauthorized disclosure of confidential matters by federal employees, isn't particularly helpful to businesses, but is something of which businesses that interact with the federal government should be aware.

Where a product imported into the United States has been made with a misappropriated trade secret, the trade secret owner may bring an action before the U.S. International Trade Commission (ITC) to bar the importation of the product under an unfair competition theory.

Trade secrets are hard to protect. The best defense against misappropriation is preventing unauthorized disclosures. One may also use Confidentiality Agreements and the like, but secrecy will always be more effective than even authorized disclosures.

PROTECTING YOUR IP

Regardless of the type of IP you're trying to protect, before taking any action which could affect your legal rights, please consult an attorney in your jurisdiction. The information in this chapter is not intended to be comprehensive, and barely scratches the surface of this important area of law.

The best thing you can do is educate yourself, and work closely with your general counsel and an IP attorney. Under no circumstances should you try to take a DIY approach to your IP legal work (or any legal work)!

CHAPTER EIGHT

THE ROLE OF ACCOUNTANTS IN YOUR BUSINESS

Accountants & Lawyers, Generally

Both accountants and lawyers have an important role to play in your business— even from the start! I should say, *especially* from the start! Those who cut corners by asking whether they should consult an accountant **or** a lawyer do themselves a disservice, because this is not an either / or question. The answer is: both!

While, all too often, lawyers or accountants try to appear to help their clients by offering advice that really is outside the bounds of their profession, lawyers and accountants **should** provide fundamentally different kinds of advice.

Knowledgeable accountants and lawyers both can provide tax advice and tax planning strategies to businesses (and individual entrepreneurs). In federal tax courts, both lawyers and certain non-lawyers—including qualified accountants— can represent clients in cases before the courts.

Nevertheless, lawyers are trained by completely different methods than accountants—methods that give them an advantage in tax litigation, appeals, and liability-related matters. These methods include, but are not limited to, studying legal writing and legal research, studying case law, and engaging in courtroom simulations (e.g. moot court, mock trial competitions, etc.) or associate practice (under the supervision of a seasoned attorney).

On the other hand, accountants have an edge in matters pertaining to financial strategy, because their training is more focused around financial planning, and understanding the nuances of tax regulations and codes (which attorneys also get, especially if they have an LL.M.[61] in tax).

As a general rule, accountants are excellent at assessing the way things are and the way things have been, or were, in the past; and, relative to tax attorneys they have a comparatively limited capacity for forecasting (i.e. planning for the future). Attorneys, on the other hand are probably the better go-to option for those seeking forward-looking advice about tax planning and strategy, with the caveat that such advice will need to be integrated into your overall financial strategy, which is something you, your tax lawyer, and your accountant should try to do together.

Remember, these general guidelines are not all-or-nothing rules! "Nearly all choices are made at the margin. That means that they almost always involve additions to (or subtractions from) current conditions, rather than "all-or-nothing" decisions."[62]

Accountants, Lawyers, and Business Formation

I will not go so far as to say that accountants have *nothing* to say or contribute to the discussion of what business organization to choose. I will say, however, that entrepreneurs far too often use accountants, instead of attorneys, as a (perceived) lower-cost provider of business formation legal services. This is a bad decision for both the client and the accountant for a number of reasons.

First, the accountant is not qualified to give legal advice. Second, and perhaps more worrisome for accountants who unwisely agree to assist clients with matters that affect their legal rights when not licensed to practice law, doing so constitutes the unauthorized practice of law, unless the accountant is also a licensed attorney. In Tennessee, the "Attorney General's Office can file civil lawsuits against individuals and companies engaged in the unauthorized practice

---

[61] A Master of Laws degree, from the Latin, *Magister Legum* or *Legum Magister*, is a postgraduate academic degree. An LL.M. is usually pursued by holders of an undergraduate law degree, professional law degree, or undergraduate degree in a related subject (e.g., *but not exclusively*, political science; one's native language; economics; history; philosophy; or psychology).

[62] (Gwartney, Stroup, Lee, Ferrarini, & Calhoun 2016)

of law. Some of these cases involve people who are not licensed attorneys but who provide legal advice for a fee and/or attempt to represent clients in court."[63]

> "NO PERSON SHALL ENGAGE IN THE PRACTICE OF LAW OR DO LAW BUSINESS, OR BOTH, AS DEFINED IN [T.C.A. § 23-3-101], UNLESS THE PERSON HAS BEEN DULY LICENSED AND WHILE THE PERSON'S LICENSE IS IN FULL FORCE AND EFFECT, NOR SHALL ANY ASSOCIATION OR CORPORATION ENGAGE IN THE PRACTICE OF THE LAW OR DO LAW BUSINESS, OR BOTH. ..."[64]

In Tennessee, "Law Business" means: "the **advising** or **counseling** for valuable consideration of any person as to any secular law, **the drawing or the procuring of or assisting in the drawing for valuable consideration of any paper, document or instrument affecting or relating to secular rights**, the doing of any act for valuable consideration in a representative capacity, **obtaining or tending to secure for any person any property or property rights whatsoever**, or the soliciting of clients directly or indirectly to provide such services."[65] (emphasis mine)

In Tennessee, the "practice of law" means: "the appearance as an advocate in a representative capacity or the drawing of papers, pleadings or documents or the performance of any act in such capacity in connection with proceedings pending or prospective before any court, commissioner, referee or any body, board, committee or commission constituted by law or having authority to settle controversies, or the soliciting of clients directly or indirectly to provide such services."[66]

In Tennessee, the unauthorized practice of law, in violation of T.C.A. § 23-3-103(a) is a Class A misdemeanor. In general, a Class A misdemeanor is punishable by up to eleven (11) months, twenty-nine (29) days in jail, or a fine of up to two thousand five hundred dollars ($2,500), or both, unless otherwise provided by

---

[63] Slattery, Herbert H. "Prosecuting the Unauthorized Practice of Law." *Tennessee State Government - TN.gov*, Tennessee Attorney General & Reporter, www.tn.gov/attorneygeneral/working-for-tennessee/prosecuting-the-unauthorized-practice-of-law.html.

[64] Tenn. Code Ann. § 23-3-103(a).

[65] Tenn. Code Ann. § 23-3-101(1).

[66] Tenn. Code Ann. § 23-3-101(3).

statute.[67] The unauthorized practice of law is an especially serious Class A misdemeanor, however, and its penalty is "otherwise provided by statute."

Tenn. Code Ann. § 23-3-103(c) provides:

(1) The attorney general and reporter may bring an action in the name of the state to restrain by temporary restraining order, temporary injunction or permanent injunction any violation of this chapter; to obtain a civil penalty in an amount not to exceed ten thousand dollars ($10,000) per violation, and to obtain restitution for any person who has suffered an ascertainable loss by reason of the violation of this chapter. The attorney general and reporter shall be entitled to be reimbursed for the reasonable costs and expenses of investigation and prosecution of acts under this chapter, including, but not limited to, reasonable attorney fees as well as expert and other witness fees.

(2) The action may be brought in a court of competent jurisdiction:

(A) In the county where the alleged violation took place or is about to take place;

(B) In the county in which the defendant resides, has a principal place of business or conducts, transacts or has conducted business; or

(C) If the defendant cannot be found in any of the locations in subdivisions (c)(2)(A) and (B), in the county in which the defendant can be found.

(3) The courts are authorized to issue orders and injunctions to restrain, prevent and remedy violations of this chapter, and the orders and injunctions shall be issued without bond.

(4) Any knowing violation of the terms of an injunction or order issued pursuant to this chapter shall be punishable by a civil penalty of not more than twenty thousand dollars ($20,000) per violation, in addition to any other appropriate relief.

---

[67] Tenn. Code Ann. § 40-35-111(e)(1).

Tenn. Code Ann. § 23-3-103(d) also provides to local bar associations a right of action to enforce the prohibition on the unauthorized practice of law.

Accountants who assist their clients with legal matters, and who thereby "do law business" as that term is defined under Tenn. Code Ann. § 23-3-101(1), risk prosecution for the unauthorized practice of law. In Tennessee, that means potential fines of up to $10,000 per violation, and jail time of up to 11 months, 29 days. It's just not worth it, folks.

For legal matters, ask a lawyer for advice. For financial matters, ask an accountant for advice. If you have both, you really can't go wrong. If you're trying to get by using just one or the other, you need to ask yourself whether or not you really can afford to do business, if you can't afford both an accountant and a lawyer. To that question, by the way, the answer is very likely, "No."

TAX ACCOUNTANTS & TAX ATTORNEYS

Ask not, "Do I need a tax attorney or an accountant?" Instead, understand why you need both a tax attorney and an accountant. Unless you have both, you are leaving yourself potentially exposed to financial and legal liability.

Tax attorneys generally have a *Juris Doctor* (J.D. or "Doctor of Laws") as well a Master of Laws (LL.M.) in Tax Law / Taxation. Certified Public Accountants (CPAs) are not attorneys (unless they are also attorneys); they are accountants who have had to pass the Uniform CPA examination. Generally speaking, attorneys focus on tax defense and strategic planning in advance to avoid the necessity of defending a client against whom the government has brought a case for tax crimes. CPAs, on the other hand, generally tend to focus on the creation of financial statements and other documents which report financial information about a person or business to interested third parties, including the IRS.

Some people find it confusing that many CPAs work in a variety of tax-related areas that often overlap with certain areas of tax attorneys' professional practice. CPAs and tax attorneys each have their own unique specializations, however; understanding these particular, exclusive proficiencies is important to understanding why you need both a tax attorney and an accountant on your business support team when tax time comes around each year.

Understanding Your CPA's Practice

A CPA HAS THE FLEXIBILITY TO WORK IN ANY AREA OF ACCOUNTING, INCLUDING AUDITING, TAXES, FINANCIAL ACCOUNTING AND REPORTING, FINANCIAL ANALYSIS AND CASH MANAGEMENT, ACCORDING TO THE AMERICAN INSTITUTE OF CPAS. CPAS WORK IN BOTH THE PUBLIC AND PRIVATE SECTOR. EARNING A CPA IMPROVES AN ACCOUNTANT'S JOB FLEXIBILITY AND CAREER ADVANCEMENT PROSPECTS, ACCORDING TO THE BUREAU OF LABOR STATISTICS. SOME ACCOUNTING POSITIONS REQUIRE A CPA TITLE. FOR INSTANCE, AN ACCOUNTANT WHO FILES A REPORT WITH THE SECURITIES AND EXCHANGE COMMISSION MUST BE A CPA.[68]

Understanding Your Lawyer's Practice

A J.D. IS DESIGNED TO PROVIDE BUDDING LAWYERS WITH A BROAD BASE OF LEGAL EDUCATION, PREPARING THEM TO FOCUS ON ANY AREA OF THE LAW. WHILE IN LAW SCHOOL, THEY CAN FOCUS THEIR EDUCATION IN PARTICULAR LEGAL SPECIALTY AREAS, SUCH AS CRIMINAL LAW, TAX LAW, LABOR LAW, ENVIRONMENTAL LAW OR CORPORATE LAW, SO THAT THEY ARE PREPARED TO CONCENTRATE THEIR PRACTICES IN THEIR CHOSEN AREA. SOME LAWYERS WHO SPECIALIZE IN ACCOUNTING AREAS, SUCH AS TAX LAW, ALSO ACQUIRE A CPA QUALIFICATION TO BURNISH THEIR CREDENTIALS. *ID.*

Also, some lawyers really go the extra mile, and get the LLM in Tax Law mentioned above. For attorneys who make that commitment, often Tax Law is all they do, and they focus on either the defense of clients against whom the government is bringing allegations of tax crimes or tax planning to help their clients reduce the likelihood of an audit or otherwise strategically optimize their tax credits and deductions.

---

[68] Gresham, T. (2013, April 20). *CPA vs. JD*. Retrieved August 11, 2015, from http://work.chron.com/cpa-vs-jd-13819.html

CPAs and Tax Attorneys: Better Together

As the Start-Ups & Small Businesses Aspect of Practice Leader for the <u>National Center for Preventive Law</u>, I talk to a lot of people who are interested in starting a new business, as well as a lot of small business owners who are seeking legal advice. One thing I notice far too often is people trying to get by using *either* an accountant *or* a tax attorney, when they should be using *both* CPAs *and* tax attorneys.

If you are an entrepreneur, if you are involved in a start-up (as a partner, company officer, or investor), or if you are a business decision-maker with close financial ties to your company, you likely need a qualified professional to prepare financial reports and documents (CPA) and a different qualified professional to help you strategically optimize your tax credits and deductions (a tax attorney).

While some, if not most, CPAs who practice in the tax area can help increase your awareness of various credits and deductions, and while they may even help you make some good decisions, their focus is usually reactive, rather than proactive. What I mean by that is that CPAs tend to look things concretely, as they are, and concern themselves with analyzing and reporting the circumstances they observe. Tax attorneys, on the other hand, tend to look at the Internal Revenue Code, with an eye towards helping their clients strategically make decisions designed to lower their tax burden and add value to their business. In this way, tax attorneys tend to take an approach based on how they believe things should be, and try to guide their clients towards that ideal.

Again, there is some overlap, here, and that's a good thing! The above statements are merely generalizations, not absolute, black-and-white statements of Gospel Truth. Also, your mileage may vary. There is surprising diversity in the marketplaces for accounting and legal services. The take-away point is: these professionals do some of the same things, but also a lot of things exclusive to their own professions; and they do what they do with largely different perspectives and goals. It is to your great advantage, therefore, to ensure you have both CPAs and tax attorneys supporting you and your business. Doing so will increase the likelihood that you are both accurately reporting your financial information to the IRS and other interested third parties, and making sound strategic business decisions that have favorable tax consequences.

CHAPTER NINE

YOUR LEADERSHIP TEAM

You should think of your leadership team as a network of overlapping partnerships all oriented towards achieving a common goal. I don't mean "partnerships" in the strictly legal sense, of course. Some of these "partners" actually will be employees. Rather, I mean "partnerships" in a looser, more colloquial sense, in the sense that each "partner's" incentives are aligned with each other "partner's" incentives, as well as those of the business you are building.

I cannot strongly enough recommend the books Daniel Priestley has written. In his book, *Key Person of Influence*, he says there are five "Ps" one needs to become a key person of influence:

1. "You need a **perfect pitch**;

2. You need to **publish** your ideas;

3. You need to "**productise**" your value;[69]

4. You need to raise your **profile**; and

5. You need great **partnerships**."[70]

At the time of this writing, you can download a copy of the Revised Edition of *Key Person of Influence*, for free, from this link: http://www.entrevo.com/downloads/Key-Person-of-Influence-Revised-Edition.pdf

Skip to Page 137. After reading that section, start back at the beginning of the book, and read the whole thing. Seriously. You'll be glad you did.

---

[69] Yes, I know "productise" isn't a word, but the concept is fairly close to what it sounds like—turn your ideas into products, or information products, which can be sold.

[70] Priestley, D. (2014). *Key Person of Influence, Revised Edition*. Rethink Press.

For more information about building such successful teams and strategic partnerships, I recommend reading the following books: *Zero to One*, by Peter Thiel; *The Culture Code*, by Daniel Coyle; and everything Daniel Priestley has written, because his books always include astute collaboration and team-building insights.

YOUR SUPPORT TEAM

Having both an accountant and a business lawyer as part of your team are essential to your success, no matter what business structure you seek to pursue. An attorney who serves as "general counsel" is the chief lawyer for a business; if that lawyer is independently contracted, and not on the business's payroll, he is said to be "outside general counsel" for the business. Outside general counsel services are crucial to a business's success, because legal services are necessary for every business, and are one area where cutting corners will usually result in expensive problems later. Taking a proactive, preventive approach to your legal issues can seem costly, but the preventive approach is often far less expensive than the alternative—litigation. You need an accountant for similar reasons. It's better to pay a reasonable amount, in advance, for bookkeeping, payroll, tax preparation, tax filing, and other accounting services than pay a lot more, later, for audits, forensic accounting services, fines, and penalties.

Insurance has the potential to be a very good thing, if utilized properly and cost-effectively. In some industries, certain kinds of insurance legally may be mandatory. In most, having some kind of insurance protection is just good business. Try to keep in mind—and consult your business attorney and accountant—how much liability protection you need for your business, and consider this when choosing your business structure. For some businesses, having adequate insurance may be an acceptable alternative to a business structure that is more expensive to form and operate.

YOUR OPERATIONS TEAM

Employees vs. Independent Contractors

Having the right people is important, but they don't necessarily need to be employees. Sometimes, the people doing the heavy lifting are independent contractors. Outsourcing is not a dirty word. Smart businesses of all sizes outsource all kinds of aspects of their business. A business can outsource its back office operations, such as accounting, payroll, human resources, customer service, marketing, and even their legal department to independent contractors.

In fact, my firm, ExecutiveLP®, provides outside general counsel and other legal services to entrepreneurs and small businesses, *as an independent contractor*.

One must be very careful, however, not to misclassify employees as independent contractors, and vice versa. Effective January 1, 2020, Tennessee adopted the federal Internal Revenue Service's 20-factor test,[71] mandating that it be used to determine whether a worker is an employee or an independent contractor under:

- The Tennessee Wage Regulation Act;

- The Tennessee Occupational Safety and Health Act;

- The Tennessee Employment Security Law; and

- The Tennessee Drug-Free Workplace Law.

Whether those tasked with carrying out your business's day-to-day work are employees, independent contractors, or—as is the case in most businesses—a mixture of both, a wise entrepreneur or small business decision-maker will elect to use written contracts for both. Many employers mistakenly believe that using a written contract will somehow change the at-will nature of employment, but this is not so. A written employment agreement simply defines the relationship between employer and employee, and sets forth the terms and conditions for employment—including the at-will nature of the employment.

It should be obvious that an independent **contract**or would use a **contract**, but an alarming number of independent contractors still do not use written contracts for their services. Failing to use a written contract to define and govern the relationship with an independent contractor is an ***invitation to litigation***. Do not make this novice mistake. Instead, have your general counsel attorney draft a contract to define and govern the relationship with each independent contractor. This is both less expensive than you probably think, and *far less expensive* than litigation in the event of a dispute.

Other Employment Law Issues

Employment law, generally is beyond the scope of this book, but it is a perennial source of questions and concerns for most small businesses. Whether you need guidance with regard to compliance with wage & hour laws, OSHA compliance,

---

[71] Tenn. Code Ann. § 50-2-111, Tenn. Code Ann. § 50-3-103, Tenn. Code Ann. § 50-7-207 and Tenn. Code Ann. § 50-9-103, as amended by 2019 Bill Text TN H.B. 539.

or the development of good policies and procedures, a general counsel attorney can help steer you in the right direction. Perhaps just as importantly, a good general counsel attorney can add real value to your business by helping you to develop business assets which will help you get the most out of your employer-employee relationships and avoid disputes. Don't neglect to add legal to your team, *first* Then, let them help you structure every other relationship your business has with anyone (e.g. owners, officers, employees, independent contractors, customers, vendors, etc).

CHAPTER TEN

YOUR BUSINESS PLAN (AND WHAT TO DO IF YOU DON'T HAVE ONE)

A business without a written business plan is like an ancient sailing ship on the high seas without a map. It might be a sunny day with wind in your sails when you start out, but a storm is coming, and you're going to get tossed around a bit. You better have a way to figure out where you are when that happens. A well-written, thorough business plan will keep you focused on your priorities. Come what may, if you have a map you can get back on course, even if you start to drift a bit as a result of rough seas.

What to Do If You're About to Launch a Business without a Business Plan

STOP! Write a business plan. There are tons of resources, out there, to help you get started. Some of the best resources I have encountered are:

1. *Successful Business Plan Secrets & Strategies, 7th edition*, by Rhonda Abrams; and

2. Bizplan or PlanGuru.

Business plan software isn't cheap, but it's a great investment. PlanGuru is pricier than Bizplan, and I like Bizplan better, but PlanGuru has some advantages, discussed below, over Bizplan—particularly for existing businesses.

Even if you decide to drop around $50 on the book by Rhonda Abrams (and I recommend doing so), you'll probably still want to get some business plan software. Unless you go with the $350 lifetime Bizplan option (not a bad idea, considering that you'll want to update your business plan from time to time), you might save some cash in the short term by getting Ms. Abrams's book, first, and getting a rudimentary business plan put together to the best of your ability, without using any software. Then, sign up for the $30/mo. Bizplan option, and use the heck out of that software for a month or two, print everything out, and then unsubscribe. This is definitely the *cheap* way to go about doing the right thing. Personally, I'd prefer to spend the $350.00, take my time, get things right, and know I can always utilize the Bizplan platform in the future when I want to update my business plan.

Of course, there are other business plan software platforms out there. I just like this one.

What to Do If You Are Operating a Business without a Business Plan

STOP FREAKING OUT! Write a business plan. You can either get a copy of the book by Rhonda Abrams, which I mentioned in the previous section or use a software platform, like PlanGuru, or both. Given the hefty price tag on PlanGuru, if you're going with the monthly option ($99/mo! Ouch!), you might want to get all the value you can squeeze out of Rhonda Abrams's book, fi rst. This could save you some time, and some moolah.

I like PlanGuru better than Bizplan for existing businesses, because PlanGuru supports importing historical results. Jonas DeMuro, writing for techradar.com, offers this insight:

> "PlanGuru is a comprehensive, and powerful software package in the business planning space. Education is provided via a series of case studies at their PlanGuru Univrsity [sic] and a whole slew of video tutorials.
>
> The feature set includes flexible budgeting that can handle a simple small business, or a larger multi-department operating budget, and financial forecasting that uses multiple methods, including intelligent and turn-key methods - twenty methods in total. Historical results can also be imported with the general ledger import utility which can then applied to produce a rolling forecast. They also offer PlanGuru Launch, a service to bring in expertise that starts at $250 per hour of assistance."

PlanGuru, while expensive, might actually be the better value for an existing business, especially if you're feeling overwhelmed, and don't mind spending money to get help writing your business plan. While $250 / hour is pretty steep for business plan-writing consulting services, if the end result is worth the investment, that's all that should matter.

Just Get Started

However you go about it, **just get started**! The SBA has business plan-writing resources. You can also reach out to the Tennessee Small Business Development Center (TSBDC) location nearest you, and ask for help. Organizations, like SCORE, will also give you help, provide mentoring, and point you in the direction of more resources.

The worst thing you can do is procrastinate. Get started, and when you do, don't forget your **BAIL** Team: **B**anking, **A**ccounting, **I**nsurance, and **L**egal! Start with Legal, then add Accounting, then Banking and Insurance. Make sure that you plan for these core relationships in your business plan, too! That means, you'll need to budget for legal and accounting services. Don't worry, there are tons of great pros out there, waiting to help you.

Good luck on your entrepreneurial journey!

GLOSSARY OF TERMS

Business. Commercial intercourse between two or more persons or legal entities.

Business Form. See "Business Organization".

Business Organization. A business's legal structure; the type of organization that operates a business (e.g. sole proprietorship, partnership, limited liability company, corporation, etc).

Corporation *de Jure*. "A corporation formed in full compliance with the laws of its governing state; it exists as a legal person for all purposes and its incorporators and shareholders will not be subject to personal liability for its obligations."[72]

Disregarded Entity. "A disregarded entity is one that is disregarded as an entity separate from its owner."[73]

Domestic Corporation. "When referred to in, or by, a particular state, a corporation (*q.v.*) created by or under the laws of the state, or located in the state and created by or under the laws of the United States." (Anderson Publishing Co. 2002)

Joint and Several Liability. The liability of two or more people, together, and individually; each person, individually, is liable, <u>and</u> all the relevant persons are, together, liable.

Legal Structure. See "Business Organization".

Limited Liability Company. "An unincorporated form of business organization, similar to a general or limited partnership but possessing a limited liability shield

---

[72] Anderson Publishing Co. (2002). *The Law Dictionary*.

[73] U.S. Treasury Dept., Internal Revenue Service. (2019, May 9). Limited Liability Company Possible Repercussions: Internal Revenue Service. Retrieved January 2, 2020, from https://www.irs.gov/businesses/small-businesses-self-employed/limited-liability-company-possible-repercussions.

that protects its owners from liability to the same extent that stockholders of a corporation are insulated from its debts and obligations." *Id.*

Partnership. Two or more persons or legal entities doing business together for profit.

"Pass Through" Entity. See "Disregarded Entity".